CONCERNING
God

CONCERNING
God

With common sense as their guide,
a preacher and a student search for the truth.

MICHAEL MENDLER

CONCERNING GOD
Copyright © 2013 by Michael Mendler

ISBN: 978-1-77069-799-7

Word Alive Press
131 Cordite Road, Winnipeg, MB R3W 1S1
www.wordalivepress.ca

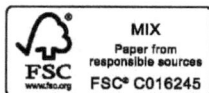

WORD ALIVE PRESS
Just Write!

MIX
Paper from
responsible sources
FSC   FSC® C016245

Library and Archives Canada Cataloguing in Publication

Mendler, Michael, 1971-

Concerning God : with common sense as their guide, a preacher and student search for the truth / Michael Mendler.

ISBN 978-1-77069-799-7

1. God (Christianity). 2. Christian life. I. Title.

BT103.M45 2012   231   C2012-908463-8

FOR TRUTH-SEEKERS.
MAY GOD, WHO IS TRUTH,
GUIDE YOU SAFELY HOME.

TABLE OF
Contents

PART ONE:
Seekers

CHAPTER ONE:
Intersection

"I suppose I'm agnostic," the student replied with a shrug. He smoothed his thick brown locks to one side and avoided looking the preacher in the eye. "I wouldn't go so far as to say there is no God; I just think there's no way of knowing for sure."

The preacher studied the young man. Like many of the students who frequented the plaza, the young man was dressed in a hoodie, jeans, and flat-soled running shoes. His dark eyes and hair added to his slightly sombre disposition.

"And if God *does* exist," the young man added cynically, "I think it's pointless to try to discover what he's really like."

"Really?" The preacher paused, trying to size up the young man's perspective. "And what makes you think that?"

"Well, just look at all the religions there are, for starters." The student's eyes darted downward, then up at the gleaming office towers of steel and glass. "Buddhism, Judaism, Christianity...everyone's got their ideas about God. Who knows which one—if any of them—is right."

The preacher leaned forward and peered intently at the young man. "I think I understand your frustration."

"Really?" The question had a mocking tone.

"Absolutely," the preacher continued, "but I happen to believe it's possible for ordinary people to discover the truth about God."

The student looked puzzled and mildly intrigued. "And how is that?"

"By relying on something most people today neglect—common sense."

The student was amused. While strolling through the plaza on his way to work, he never would have imagined being drawn into a conversation about God by an aging preacher he had only just met. The pizzeria where he worked was a twenty-minute walk from his home on the west side, just long enough that he'd decided to sit down for a rest. The older gentleman next to him on the park bench had been dressed in slacks and dress shirt, a sandwich in his hand. Judging by his graying hair and the furrows over his brow, he was in his late fifties.

The man had asked if he was a student, then inquired about his studies.

"I'm an undergrad in my third year of psychology at the university," he replied. Truth be told, he was in his fourth year, but owing to changing his major (yet again), he still had a year remaining.

The man then revealed that he was pastor of a nearby church and began to inquire about his religious background and beliefs.

He explained to the stranger that he had no religious upbringing to speak of, and tried to articulate his current beliefs, which was difficult; like many things in his life, they were in a constant state of flux.

Though initially irritated by the preacher's questions and attempts to engage him in conversation, the discussion had become interesting. After a time, he felt his defenses lower.

"Common sense?" he asked.

"That's right. In fact, I think it's reasonable to assume that not much more than common sense would be required."

The student smiled wryly, thinking of the philosophers he had studied. *Sorry fellas*, he thought. *Sounds like you've been trying too hard.*

"And why is that?" he replied.

"Because otherwise God would only be accessible to people with special knowledge or education. And I think that's impractical—not to mention unfair." The preacher paused. "The Bible says God isn't far from any one of us. I happen to believe that's true."

The student chuckled. "Right. But you're a Christian, so of course you believe that."

"I don't believe it just because I'm a Christian," the preacher replied matter-of-factly.

"I believe it because it makes sense."

"But you can't even prove God exists in the first place," the student pointed out.

The preacher smiled. "Well, if we're going to talk about *proof*, we may not get very far at all." He glanced upward. Overhead, a commercial jet traced a silent path across the cloudless sky. "It's probably impossible to *prove* God exists, at least in any absolute sense. But I think we can make some common sense assumptions about where the truth of God might be found. That may help narrow down the options."

The student looked suspicious, uncertain. The preacher recognized the look. It was the look of someone standing at the cliff's edge.

"That is," the preacher added cautiously, "if you're serious about wanting to find some answers."

The student's eyes betrayed his mistrust. "I want to know the truth," he said slowly. "But don't expect that you'll talk me into becoming a Christian."

"Fair enough," the preacher replied. "In fact, I wouldn't want to *talk* you into anything. All I'm saying is, we can discuss it and you can decide for yourself what you think."

The student pulled his cell phone out of his pants pocket. He only had a few minutes to traverse the three blocks to the pizzeria before his shift began.

"If you want, we could get together again another time," the preacher offered.

The student's initial reaction was to decline, but his curiosity had been aroused, both by the preacher's frank manner and keen intellect. He was surprised to discover the latter in a person with deep religious convictions, and especially in a preacher.

"Alright, I'm game," he replied after a moment. "When do you want to meet?"

The preacher held up his half-eaten sandwich. "I'm here everyday during the week, same time."

The student thought for a moment. The summer semester started the following week, but he had Fridays off. "I'm free on Fridays."

The preacher nodded. "Then let's make it Friday, lunch-time. I look forward to seeing you." The preacher extended his hand.

The student stood and shook it, smiling somewhat sheep-ishly. "Yeah ... Uh, me too."

As the young man strode quickly across the plaza, the preacher wondered if he would see him again. People had a way of feigning interest in the truth until they were challenged to a real discussion. He had once been such a student himself. Time would tell.

As the student walked away, a wave of dread swept over him. Part of him suspected the preacher intended to use their discussion as an opportunity to push Christianity on him, or get him to church. But another, deeper part longed for real answers.

In fact, he had taken several philosophy courses as electives, believing he would benefit from being in the company of fellow truth-seekers. But all he seemed to have learned so far was that the world was full of contradictory opinions, and even his professors were reluctant to say what was truth. Not exactly promising...

As he turned south and spied the pizzeria among the cluster of restaurants lining the street, the aroma of garlic and freshly baked bread distracted him from considerations of the human and the divine. Whatever secrets the universe held, he was glad pizza wasn't one of them.

CHAPTER TWO:
Assumptions

The following Friday found the preacher in his usual spot, on a bench near the centre of the plaza, facing the financial district. He'd spent most of the morning preparing his next sermon and his mind was still preoccupied as he unwrapped his sandwich and surveyed the plaza.

Located in the centre of the city—and dotted with sculptures, benches, and fountains—the plaza was a favourite gathering place for people from every walk of life.

Businessmen and women could be found sitting on benches, sipping coffee and typing on their laptops and smartphones. Mothers pushing strollers congregated to talk and enjoy the sun. With the university campus only a few blocks away, there were always students munching fries from the Chip Wagon, listening to music, or sleeping in the sun. Joggers and rollerbladers wearing earbuds, oblivious to the throng, occasionally wove their way through the sea of pedestrians on their way to destinations unknown.

The busyness was what the preacher loved most. Somehow in the middle of all this human activity, surrounded by the ever-present rumble of the city, he could lose himself. His lunchtime ritual also gave him a chance to reflect and pray, something he deeply appreciated—and sorely missed when the cold weather eventually forced him indoors. Although the church he pastored was located a mere block from the plaza, whenever he sat on his favourite bench he felt as if he were a thousand miles away...

"Hey."

The words startled the preacher. He turned to see the student, backpack in hand. He felt a stab of guilt as he realized their planned meeting had entirely slipped his mind.

The student smiled weakly and sat heavily on the bench beside him. He was visibly nervous. If the preacher remembered correctly, he was wearing the same clothes—ripped jeans and brown hoodie—he'd worn the previous Friday.

"You remembered!" the preacher exclaimed. He was genuinely surprised and delighted to see the young man.

"Yeah, but beware—I'm full of objections."

The preacher chuckled. "Objections to what?"

"To whatever you're going to say," the student replied. "I'm a great debater."

"Well then," the preacher said, welcoming the challenge, "we should have some fun, because so am I."

The sun poked out from between the great white pillows of cloud drifting lazily overhead, warming their neck and shoulders. The effect was welcome; it was still early in the summer and the air hadn't fully cast off the chill of spring.

"So where do we start?" the young man asked. He crossed his arms and leaned back, trying his best to seem at ease.

The preacher tried to recall the content of their previous conversation. His mind was still cluttered with thoughts about his upcoming sermon.

"We were talking about how to narrow down the options," he said. "And I suggested we could make some common sense assumptions."

"Right. So, what kind of assumptions are we talking about?"

The preacher considered how best to begin. Suddenly, the theologian in him kicked into gear. "Well, if we're going to search for the truth about God, we should probably define who it is we're talking about."

"Okay." The student understood from his philosophy classes that this was known as "defining terms."

"By *God*, I mean a Being who is omnipotent, omnipresent, and good."

The student was familiar with the terms. "But why do we need to define God in that particular way?" he retorted. "How do we know that He, or *She*, is any of those things?"

The preacher smiled. *This is going to be interesting*, he mused.

"Actually, that's a very good question," the preacher replied. "But I think we can assume those three qualities about God because they're self-evident, defining qualities. If we're talking about a Being without those attributes, then we're not talking about God. But if we're asking questions about the existence of God, by implication we're asking about the existence of an all-powerful, omnipresent Being—the Being who created the universe. Otherwise, I don't think we really have a discussion."

The student thought for a moment, his head tilted sceptically. At the same time, the preacher noticed a piece of lint clinging to the young man's sparse but scraggly facial hair. He smiled inwardly.

Do these kids ever shave or comb their hair? he wondered.

"I'm not sure I agree with that," the student responded. "I think we could define God in any number of ways. Why assume He's good, for instance? Doesn't the world reflect what you—as a Christian—would call good and evil? And if so, couldn't God be evil, or both evil *and* good?"

"Well, I suppose He could be," the preacher replied. True to his word, the young man seemed determined to challenge him at every opportunity. "But if we can't assume God is good, we also can't assume He would have good intentions toward us. And in that case, knowing the truth about God probably wouldn't do us much good." He paused to let the young man absorb the thought. "But I think we're *having* this discussion because we believe there's some value in knowing the truth about God. Besides, if God isn't good, why create the universe—or us—at all? And what about beauty and pleasure?"

"Or famine and injustice?" the student countered.

"Touché. But the existence of good and evil doesn't imply that they're both reflective of God's nature. The reality is we could spend all day raising questions about the nature of God, but I'm not sure that would—"

"I don't object to raising more questions," the student interjected.

"Neither do I," the preacher replied, "unless they lead us out of the realm of common sense. I'm simply saying I think it's reasonable to assume that God, if He exists, is good. And if He isn't, I suspect that should become evident at some point—and we can cross that bridge when we come to it."

"Alright, so we'll assume He's good. What's next?"

"Well, the first assumption we could make is that God created humanity for a purpose."

The student considered the statement, reflecting on what he'd learned in his philosophy classes. He shrugged. "Why a purpose? The existentialists would say that existence precedes essence, that we have no inherent purpose, which is why we're so miserable."

The preacher nodded. "Right, but we're considering the possibility that we were *created*. If our existence is merely the product of chance forces in a chaotic universe, humanity *has* no purpose, but if God created us, it only makes sense to believe He made us for a *reason*."

The student shrugged. "I don't know. What if we're just a whim, or some kind of experiment?"

"Well, if God is good, I think it's safe to assume that He didn't create us on a whim. And even if we *were* an experiment we would still have a purpose. Being an experiment isn't much of a purpose, but it still qualifies. In any case, we're not talking yet about what the purpose *is*. I'm just saying it makes sense to believe we have one."

"So even if our purpose sucks, we still have a purpose."

The preacher chuckled. "I guess that's one way to put it. And if there is no God, all bets are off."

"Fair enough." The student's anxiety was fading. He was surprised at the preacher's open-mindedness and willingness to deal with his objections.

"Now, here's where it begins to get interesting." The preacher paused, his eyes betraying a hint of excitement. "It's also reasonable to assume God would be willing to communicate that purpose to us."

The student looked unconvinced. "Why is that? Why should we assume God would tell us what our purpose is? I mean, what if He wants us to figure it out for ourselves?"

"That's certainly a possibility," the preacher replied, "but it's not the most reasonable one. Think about it. Does it really make sense to believe God would create us and then intentionally withhold our purpose from us? Why leave us in the dark about the single most important piece of information we could possibly possess? It would be like making us a lock while withholding the key."

"Not if the *search* for our purpose was the point," the student countered. "God might withhold our purpose because it's the *search* for truth that really matters."

"I'm sorry." The preacher shook his head. "But I'll have to strongly part ways with you here. I realize that point of view is popular in academic circles, but it's really illogical."

The student felt a twinge of embarrassment at the reference to academia. He knew that his last statement reflected the opinion of some of his professors and fellow students—which he didn't actually believe.

The preacher continued. "It's like saying it's the search for food that matters, and not eating. Or the search for love that matters, and not *finding* it. Common sense tells us that our desires exist to *lead* us somewhere. The point of hunger is to eat—not to be hungry." The preacher spoke quickly. It was clear this was something he was passionate about. "Our desires have a goal, and it's in the goal that we find fulfillment. There's value in the journey, yes, but only because there's somewhere we need to go. A destination."

The student reflected in silence for a moment. "But what if our purpose is to search for truth? To be seekers?"

"To search for something that will always be withheld, or doesn't exist?" the preacher asked. "How could that result in anything but hopelessness? It sounded like you were wrestling with that last week when you expressed frustration about how to know the truth about God."

The student shrugged. "I suppose."

The preacher shook his head. "I don't think it would be consistent with the nature of a benevolent God to create us and then doom us to unfulfillment." The preacher paused, not wanting to be overly forceful. After many years in ministry, he was conscious of his occasional tendency to inadvertently bulldoze others with his convictions. "I realize the argument isn't airtight. But again, we're talking about what's reasonable, and what agrees with common sense."

The student had another thought. "But what if God isn't *able* to communicate our purpose to us?"

"What do you mean?"

"Well, what if God has been trying to communicate our purpose to us, but we can't understand what He's saying?" The student knew this was also a common view— strangely enough, among his religious friends.

"I got you. The human and ant analogy." The preacher smiled. A thinker by nature, he loved to be challenged intellectually and have the opportunity to express his opinions on subjects to which he had devoted a great deal of thought. Only rarely did such opportunities arise within the context of his work as a pastor. His congregation consisted primarily of two groups—older folks, who had settled such questions long ago, and the disadvantaged, who were preoccupied with more practical concerns. It was refreshing to converse with someone on a more abstract level.

"God's like a human being trying to talk to an ant," the preacher explained, "and we can't possibly understand Him because He doesn't speak our language."

"Exactly! I mean, if we could hear God so well, why is everyone so confused about what He's saying? Buddhists say they're hearing one thing, Muslims and Christians are hearing something else..." He shook his head. "It's so insane!"

The preacher nodded in affirmation. "Excellent question. And a good point. There is definitely some confusion about what God's saying—no disagreement there. But to believe God is somehow *incapable* of communicating to us in a way we can understand isn't really logical, either. Remember, if God exists, He's all-powerful. He must be in order to have created the universe. So to suggest He couldn't find a way to speak to us at our level would imply His power is limited in some way. Surely, if He had the ability to create the universe—and human beings—he could find a way to talk to us."

The student remained unconvinced. "But if God *can* talk to us, why aren't people hearing the same thing?"

"Interesting you should say that, actually," the preacher replied. "A lot of people claim to believe He *has* said the same thing to Buddhists and Muslims and everyone else—that all religions are basically alike. That's the view of Hinduism, more or less. But anyone who's intellectually honest would have to admit that the religions of the world are contradictory, both in their depiction of God and of His requirements for humanity."

"I'm not sure I buy that," the student replied. "What if they're all saying basically the same thing from their own perspective?"

"Not possible." the preacher stated flatly. "When you compare various religions in terms of even their most basic practices and beliefs, the differences are just too great to reconcile. How would you reconcile, for example, religions that practice human sacrifice with those that condemn such acts as pure evil? Or religions that are polytheistic with those that are fiercely monotheistic? And what about religions that believe in reincarnation versus those that believe in an eternal afterlife? Does it really make sense to believe they're basically alike when their beliefs and systems of worship are contradictory—even antagonistic—at the most fundamental levels?"

A little stunned at the soundness of the preacher's logic, the student was slow to respond. "But what if God is painting a picture of himself through *all* world religions? Like a mosaic, where each of them has just one piece of the puzzle."

The preacher shrugged. "It's an appealing idea, but not at all practical. After all, how would we know which aspect of each religion was right or wrong? And besides, if that were the case, shouldn't we have figured it out already? Why the persistent confusion about God?"

"But what about the *similarities* between different religions?" the student asked. "If only one of them is right, why would there be any similarities at all? I mean, doesn't the fact that there are similarities suggest that they all have some knowledge of the truth?"

"Yes, I believe you're correct."

The student looked surprised. "So you're saying most religions are wrong, but *some* of what they believe is right?"

The preacher nodded. His back was beginning to stiffen, so he leaned back and stretched out his legs.

"I think it makes sense to believe that some basic knowledge of God would be discernible to people without any divine revelation at all—even to non-religious people. The Bible says that creation itself reflects God's attributes and nature. I think that's not only likely; it's inevitable. After all, how could the physical universe not bear the fingerprints of the One who created it?"

"So, as a Christian, you don't have any problem believing that people who aren't Christians know something about God?"

"Not at all," the preacher replied. "I believe God has designed everything to testify to the truth and draw people to Him. But that doesn't mean all religions are the same, or equally valid. Logically speaking, nearly all religions contain very serious errors about God and it's imperative that people know the truth."

"But if God has revealed the truth to us, why do people claim to have heard such different things?"

"Well, we have our part to play in the communication process as well. Human beings are famous for hearing what we want to hear, so our confusion isn't necessarily proof that God hasn't spoken. It's just evidence of our human fickleness."

"So we're back to the original question: how do we know which religion is right?" The young man sighed. It seemed as if they were talking in circles and not making any progress at all.

The preacher perceived the young man's frustration, but he knew the issues they were discussing required careful thought and wouldn't be easily resolved. He took a breath.

"Well, I hope we're moving in that direction," the preacher said. "And our next assumption should help us out, which is that God would be able to preserve the revelation of His purpose over time."

The student repeated the statement slowly in his mind. "What do you mean by the revelation of his purpose?"

"Revelation is a theological term," the preacher explained. "Practically speaking, it refers to the record of what a group of people believe is God's Word—or communication—to them. The Bible is one example. Christians believe the Bible is God's revelation to man. Muslims regard the Koran as the Word of God, and other religions have their own holy books as well."

The student nodded. "I get that part, but... what's the assumption again?" He ran his hand through his hair, embarrassed by his difficulty following the preacher's train of thought. He had entered the conversation imagining he could think circles around the aging preacher, but was being shown otherwise.

"That God would be able to preserve the revelation of his purpose over time," the preacher repeated. "Let me explain it like this. A common argument is that God may have spoken to humanity at some point in time, but that His message has been twisted and corrupted by human beings. As a result, we no longer have a record of any pure communication from God." He paused. "You could then argue that it's impossible to know the truth about God because the truth has been corrupted. But what I'm saying is that if God told us our purpose at some point in history, it makes sense to believe that God would be able to preserve the *record* of that purpose from any human attempts to corrupt it."

"So you're saying that God would stop people from messing with the Bible, for instance."

"Yes and no. I don't mean God would necessarily *stop* people from corrupting what He'd said. I'm simply saying that He would have the ability—and clearly the desire—to preserve its purity, in spite of any attempts to alter it. To suggest that He wouldn't be able to do so would again imply that His power is limited."

The student was beginning to see the preacher's point more clearly. "In other words, why take the trouble to reveal truth to us and then allow the truth to be distorted or destroyed?"

"Exactly!" the preacher affirmed. "It wouldn't make sense."

The preacher paused and looked at his watch, surprised to see how much time had passed since their discussion began. He had been vaguely aware that his allotted lunch hour had come and gone, which wasn't a problem since his schedule was relatively flexible, but there was a board meeting in twenty minutes he couldn't afford to miss.

"Do you have to be somewhere?" The student was surprised by his own disappointment that their conversation might be drawing to an end.

"No, not just yet," the preacher replied. "I think we've got time for one more assumption." If he showed up a few minutes late, the board could begin without him.

"Okay, shoot."

"Well, our next assumption would be that a large portion of humanity would eventually be drawn to a true revelation from God."

The student digested the thought. "Mmm, I'm not sure about that one. As you said, people hear what they want to hear. How could we assume that a lot of people would even recognize a true message from God?"

"That's a good point," the preacher replied thoughtfully. "I think a lot of them wouldn't. But understand that a true revelation from God—a revelation of our purpose—would contain the answer to mankind's deepest questions and longings. If that's true, I think it only makes sense to believe that over time many people would come to recognize the significance of that revelation."

The student was unconvinced. "Perhaps. It's really hard to say, though. You would think *some* people would recognize a true message from God, but I don't know. And what if some tribe of pygmies in the Amazon have a true revelation from God and no one else even knows about it?"

The preacher laughed so loudly and abruptly that the student was startled.

"What's so funny?" the young man asked, feeling painfully self-conscious.

"Pygmies! How is it that pygmies always seem to find their way into conversations about God?" the preacher asked rhetorically. He quickly composed himself. "Sorry, I guess you'd have to be a preacher to appreciate that. Go on with what you were saying."

The student struggled to pick up his previous train of thought. "Well, that's it. I mean… I think it's possible some religious group or other could have the truth, but what if they're some tiny, isolated group somewhere—or some religion from the past. Like, what if the Greeks had it right all along?"

The student suppressed a smile. Though the Greeks weren't the most likely candidates for religious truth, they came quickly to mind, owing to his having completed a course in Greek history the previous semester.

"Ah, Zeus and Apollo!" the preacher exclaimed.

"Right, and Aphrodite—and her temple prostitutes." The young man grinned, his embarrassment quickly fading. He had learned about the various forms of worship practiced by the Greeks. Owing to its absurdity, the ritual of engaging in sex with temple prostitutes was his personal favourite.

The preacher laughed good-naturedly. "Right. A very likely candidate."

"No, I mean it. How would we know?" the student continued, a note of seriousness returning to his voice. "Maybe not the Greeks, but there are a lot of others."

"Well, as I've said before," the preacher replied, "it's possible, but not likely. I'm simply saying that if God has spoken to humanity, it makes sense to believe an increasing number of people would recognize it. History demonstrates, I think, that the truth eventually surfaces, regardless of how many lies it competes against."

The student considered the statement. *Is it really possible to know the truth with certainty?* he wondered. It seemed that everywhere he looked, he found only confusion. No one—not his professors, his friends, or anyone else—seemed to have the answers to the really important questions. The realization that everyone was so busy living life without even knowing why they were *here* in the first place was sometimes overwhelming.

"But what if God hasn't spoken yet?" the student asked. "What if He intends to speak at some point in the *future*? Then all the religions, past and present, would be wrong."

"True," the preacher replied, nodding. "But I don't think that agrees with common sense. If we can agree that God wouldn't willfully keep mankind in the dark about who He is and what our purpose is, it's almost *unimaginable* to believe that He hasn't already spoken. Think about it. If He hasn't spoken to humanity yet, with thousands of years of human history behind us, then He *has* kept us in the dark."

"So you're saying *some* religion has the truth about God."

"I think it makes sense to believe that's true."

"And you believe it's Christianity."

The preacher chuckled. "That's true—otherwise I wouldn't be a Christian." He shrugged. "But my belief doesn't make it so."

"True."

"And I'm not trying to prove right now that Christianity is the true religion. I'm simply saying that I think it's reasonable to assume that one of the religions of the world has the truth. And based on what we just discussed, I think there's a good chance it's one of the *major* religions of the world."

"So which ones are we talking about?" the student inquired. Although he wouldn't have liked to admit it, he knew his knowledge of world religions was sketchy at best.

"Well, in terms of the number of adherents, the world's leading religions are Christianity, Islam, Hinduism, and Buddhism."

The student was somewhat surprised. He wasn't sure which religions he expected the preacher to name, but the compactness of the list was unexpected.

"So those four have the largest number of followers?"

"By all estimates," the preacher replied, "roughly two-thirds of humanity profess to be followers of one of those four religions, and the numbers drop off sharply after Buddhism. All other religions, plus agnostics and atheists, make up the last third. I think it's likely one of those four has the truth. At the very least, they represent a logical starting point for our search."

The student pondered the implication of the preacher's statement. With one assumption, they had narrowed the possibilities down from hundreds, perhaps thousands of religions to four. It was a bold leap, indeed.

"And to simplify things a little further," the preacher added, "we can rule out Buddhism before we go any further, because Buddhism isn't a religion about God."

The student's surprised turned to shock. "Are you serious?"

"Absolutely," the preacher affirmed. "Buddhists don't even need to strictly believe there is a God. Their religion is primarily about discovering peace through surrendering desire within one's self. It doesn't concern God, nor does it claim to possess a revelation from God."

"Wow. Why didn't I know that?" the student asked, half-incredulous, half-amused.

"How many Buddhists are there in the world?"

"I think somewhere in the neighbourhood of three to four hundred million."

Four hundred million, the student thought to himself. It was a staggering number.

"But wouldn't the large number of followers suggest it might be the truth?" The student was struggling to believe the possibilities could be so easily reduced to four. And now, with another swift stroke, the preacher had dismissed a religion with four hundred million followers.

"Well, yes—if God *doesn't* exist," the preacher replied. "But if God exists, he certainly wouldn't have founded a religion that disregarded his own existence. Common sense demands we rule it out. Besides, we aren't saying that a large number of people wouldn't be drawn to other systems of belief. We're simply saying that, in time, the truth should attract a large number of followers."

The student looked out at the throng of people in the crowded plaza. There were so many people in the world... could so many of them really be wrong?

The preacher glanced at his watch again. It was five minutes to two. He felt a small stab of guilt for dallying so long. He would likely be late. The food bank's monthly board meeting was one of his least favourite tasks, but an important one. Finances for the food bank were a chronic challenge, and the board had to be inventive to ensure the shelves remained stocked.

"Afraid I'm going to have to call it quits for today, as I have an appointment in a few minutes," the preacher confessed. "But I would love to meet again and continue our discussion—if you're interested."

"Sure."

The student's swift response surprised them both.

"Okay, how about next Friday, same time?"

"Sounds good." The student spied the preacher's half-eaten sandwich on the bench next to him. "Sorry if I kept you from your lunch."

"Not at all," the preacher said with a smile. He held out his hand and the student shook it somewhat awkwardly. "I enjoyed our talk."

"Me too."

"See you next week."

CHAPTER THREE:
Reservations

I n the days that followed, the student reflected on his first two meetings with the aging preacher. The preacher was easier to talk to than expected; he wasn't at all stuffy or dated as he had imagined, and despite the large span of years and experience separating them, they conversed almost as peers—a fact that was as surprising as it was inexplicable.

But something was troubling him: the assumptions. In his mind, they recalled conversations that had taken place in his philosophy class, discussions that grew more dizzying and uncertain as supposition piled upon supposition. Although he was intrigued by the idea of appealing to common sense, he'd begun to question the wisdom of moving forward with so little to stand on. Unable to shake his uneasiness by the following week, he decided to be upfront with his concerns at the onset of their next meeting.

"Okay, I have a problem."

The preacher looked up from his lunch, surprised by the abrupt greeting. The air was cool and the sky was overcast, despite the fact that it had been officially summer for two weeks.

"Okay, shoot."

The student sat down quickly. "I think we're building a house of cards here."

The preacher couldn't immediately guess the young man's meaning, but sensed the deep concern behind his statement. "What do you mean exactly?"

"Well," the student continued, "our entire conversation so far has been built upon a series of assumptions we can't prove. In philosophy, we call them suppositions." He paused and the preacher nodded. "The problem with building an argument on a series of suppositions is that if any one of them are wrong, the whole argument falls apart."

"Like a house of cards," the preacher added.

"Right!"

A strange look of pleasure stole over the preacher's face. "I totally agree."

The student was surprised by the preacher's acknowledgment. "You do?"

"Absolutely. But unfortunately, there's no other way to proceed."

The student's surprise turned to bewilderment. "What do you mean? Why can't we be guided by things we can prove? By facts."

"Well, I would be game for that. What facts would we be talking about here?"

The student thought for a moment. "I don't know… scientific facts, I guess. Things that aren't in the realm of speculation. Things that are provable."

"Such as?"

"I don't know… like the fact that the earth is round."

The preacher nodded. "I see. And how do you know that it's round?"

The student looked puzzled, then amused. "Are you serious?"

"Absolutely. How do you know?"

"Well, it's been proven. Mathematically, I suppose. I mean, we have pictures that *show* it's round. There's all kind of proof."

He couldn't imagine where the preacher was headed with this line of questioning.

"Perhaps. But have you ever seen the curvature of the earth for yourself?"

The student laughed. "I'm not sure. I don't think so."

"So you've never been to space?"

"No—but what does that matter?" the student replied with a note of irritation and amusement. *This preacher is one strange character*, he thought.

"So what you're saying is, you've never seen that the world is round—but you're willing to take other people's word for it."

The student smirked. "Well, I suppose. What's your point?"

"That you don't have absolute proof. But you don't doubt that it's round. Correct?"

"True, but it's been proven by others."

"So you believe."

The student was becoming agitated. "Are you saying that you don't believe the earth is round?"

"No, what I'm pointing out is that you've formed a belief about the world on the basis of certain evidence—but not because it has been proven in an absolute sense. True?"

The student shook his head. "I don't see where you're going with this."

"I'm simply pointing out the uncertain nature of facts."

The student folded his arms. "Alright, and what if I went for a ride in the space shuttle and saw the curvature of the earth for myself? Wouldn't *that* constitute proof?"

"I don't know. How could you be certain that when you saw it, you weren't dreaming or hallucinating?"

The student's mouth dropped open. The question seemed absurd until he recalled that they'd discussed this very subject in philosophy class—the nature of reality.

"Or," the preacher continued, "that what you perceived with your eyes was an accurate reflection of reality?"

The student responded with the conclusion they had come to in class: "I guess you can't know. Not absolutely."

"My point exactly. What I'm getting at is that there's an element of faith involved in everything we believe."

The student was surprised to hear the word *faith* enter the conversation. Suddenly, a knowing look came over his face.

"Ah, I see." He nodded. "You want me to believe in God by faith, right?"

The preacher's gaze was level and direct. "Actually, what I'm saying is that whatever it is you *already* believe, you believe *that* by faith."

The student looked sceptical. "I disagree. I don't mean any disrespect, but I don't live my life by blind faith like religious people do. They just believe what they're told. I believe people should think for themselves."

"Well, I might feel disrespected just a little bit if you think my faith in God is blind." The preacher suppressed a smile. "The Bible certainly doesn't say anything about *blind* faith. Blind faith is foolish, but faith itself is inescapable."

"I don't see how that's so."

"Well, in our first discussion you said that you didn't know if God existed because you didn't feel there was sufficient proof. Is that true?"

"More or less."

"But you do have beliefs about yourself and the universe, right?"

"Naturally."

"Right, naturally. What I'm saying is that whatever you believe about those things, I'm certain you don't have absolute proof. Nevertheless, you've chosen to believe it."

The student paused to reflect. "Well, that's probably true. But I've thought a lot about what I believe, and I'm open to changing my beliefs. I don't just choose to believe what someone else tells me."

"Like religious people do."

"Right."

"Let me say something about beliefs and you can tell me if you agree. First of all, I don't think *anything* can be proven with absolute certainty." He paused, considering how to best proceed. He decided to appeal to the student's interest in philosophy. "Are you familiar with René Descartes?"

"Sure."

"Then you're probably familiar with the *Cogito*?"

"Of course. 'I think, therefore I am.'"

"Right, it was Descartes' first principle of philosophy. One of the ideas expressed in the *Cogito* is that in order to have a meaningful discussion about anything, you need a starting place. That starting place is a basic assumption—namely, that you exist. The reason that's important is that we can't really even prove with certainty the basic reality that we exist! For all we know, everything we experience in life could be a dream or a hallucination. We could be *non*-existent. Of course, we won't get very far in life if we believe that."

The student more or less agreed with the preacher's point. But not wanting to appear conciliatory, he remained silent.

"But Descartes thought there was good evidence to believe that we exist—the fact that we can *think* and wonder about our own existence," the preacher said. "It's not an ironclad proof, but it makes sense, doesn't it? It underscores the fact that we can't know *anything* with absolute certainty, and that at the most basic level life involves an element of faith."

"But Descartes wasn't talking about God," the student pointed out.

"Neither am I, at the moment," the preacher replied. "I'm talking about everyday life. The fact is, we make decisions and form beliefs all the time on the basis of incomplete evidence. An absence of proof. We can't live any other way."

The student wasn't sure how to respond. He had never regarded faith as having any value at all. He considered it a crutch for the weak, for people who were unable to think for themselves. In that respect, it even seemed dangerous. But a necessary part of life? The idea seemed absurd.

"Descartes seemed to recognize that some things must be assumed or believed as a matter of course. That faith—although he didn't use that word—is woven into the very fabric of life," the preacher continued. "As a result, the best we can do in this life is examine whatever evidence we see around us and then make judgments accordingly. That's essentially what the Bible asks us to do with respect to God. The Bible defines faith as believing in what we cannot see. Which is another way of saying what we cannot *prove*."

"So you're saying we can't be sure about anything—including God."

"Not absolutely sure, because there's always room for questions, and doubt. But that shouldn't—and doesn't—stop us from making decisions and forming beliefs about many things, including God. But if we're wise, we'll carefully examine the evidence before choosing what we believe."

The student thought for a moment. "Okay, I'll buy that. I suppose that's more or less true." A moment of silence passed as he realized he had nothing to add.

The preacher sensed the need to connect their observation to the student's original question, so they wouldn't get lost in abstractions.

"To answer your concern about building a house of cards," the preacher said, "it's true that we don't have any *proof* that our assumptions are true. But that doesn't mean they aren't good assumptions—or that we shouldn't proceed. And remember, the premise of our conversation at the onset was that God ought to be accessible to ordinary people, so the truth of God shouldn't contradict common sense."

Absorbed in thought, the student was only half-listening. *It's true*, he thought. *Some kind of leap of faith is unavoidable, no matter what you believe. Even the atheists I know can't prove God doesn't exist.*

"I see your point," he admitted. "I think you're right. There's going to be an element of faith involved no matter how we proceed." Feeling awkward, he changed the subject. "But to backtrack a bit, you said that you're faith isn't blind. What did you mean by that?"

"What I meant was that I carefully considered the evidence for the Christian faith before I chose to believe it."

"Really? So you didn't believe the Bible just because it's the Bible?"

"Mmm… something like that. I came to the realization over time that there were a lot of reasons to believe what the Bible said and taught—historical reasons, intellectual reasons, common sense reasons. As well as reasons of conscience…"

The student's interest was piqued. "Such as?"

"Well, I think we'll get ahead of ourselves if we go there right now." The preacher checked his watch. A full afternoon of administration and study awaited him and it was time to head back to the office.

The preacher felt a vague sense of disappointment at having spent so much time simply justifying the value of their discussion, but he recognized it was important to respond to the young man's concerns if their discussion were to continue.

"Looks like we'll have to stop for today," he said after a moment. "I have some work back at the church that won't go away until I do it."

The student looked surprised. "Oh, okay. Sure. I forget not everybody has the day off like me." He paused. "You want to keep going?"

"Love to—if you're interested. How's Friday next week?"

"Good, I think."

"Excellent. To be continued then. I look forward to seeing you." The preacher held out his hand.

Still not accustomed to the preacher's frank manner, he felt a twinge of embarrassment.

"Yeah. Me too."

CHAPTER FOUR:
Chrysalids

The following Sunday, the preacher mentioned his meetings with the student during his sermon. As he related some of the details of their discussion to his congregation, he was surprised by a peculiar mixture of sadness and joy. Normally articulate, he suddenly found himself stumbling over words, having difficulty expressing his thoughts. Hurriedly wrapping up his sermon, he dismissed the congregation and struggled to compose himself.

His wife, who had been listening with great interest to her husband's account of his conversations with the young man, picked up on his emotional confusion. After the service, she approached him and placed her hand gently on his shoulder.

"Sounds like you've made a friend," she said quietly.

The preacher looked at his wife. Her eyes were faintly red, as if about to fill with tears.

"Yes, well, I really hope I can help him," he replied. "He seems like a truthseeker."

"That's not what I meant."

She looked at him lovingly and kissed him on the cheek.

<hr/>

"Why don't we pick up where we left off and see where we end up," the preacher suggested.

Although usually sombre, the student seemed to be in a cheerful mood. He had arrived with two Starbucks coffees, and though the preacher normally drank decaf he accepted the coffee gratefully. The day was clear and sunny and the sun was already growing hot. The plaza was more crowded than usual with people who had made their way outdoors to enjoy the sun. Summer had finally arrived.

"Sounds good," the young man replied cheerfully.

"I believe we'd come to the conclusion that the world's main religions represented a logical starting point in our search for truth."

"Right. So we need to research world religions?"

"Not necessarily, although we could certainly do that. The reality is most people won't bother." The preacher took a sip of his coffee. As he suspected, it was syrupy and overly strong.

I'll pay for that later, he mused.

"I believe we may already know enough about each to make some very general observations," he continued. "I also think it's important to point out that the approach we're taking is an intellectual one. I don't think truth is apprehended exclusively by our intellect, but intellectual people like you and me," he cast a sideways glance at the young man, "tend to find this path an important one."

The student sipped his coffee. "So you think there are other ways to discover the truth about God?"

"Certainly," the preacher replied. "People can understand with their heart even if they don't understand with their mind."

Understand with your heart? The student pondered the meaning of the preacher's statement. "How so?"

"Well, take love or mercy, for instance," the preacher replied. "I don't know that we can fully comprehend love or mercy *intellectually*, but we don't dismiss them as illusions simply because they're difficult to rationalize. We understand them with our heart, not our head."

"I suppose," the student replied. On a bench nearby, a tired-looking man—homeless, judging by his shabby clothes and overstuffed knapsack—was feeding pigeons with some crusty bread he'd pulled out of a crumpled brown paper bag.

"And for our next assumption…" The preacher broke off, looking up. "Excuse me for a moment."

Without waiting for a response, he stood and slowly approached the man feeding pigeons. Seeing the preacher, the man grinned widely, deep lines etching his tanned face. The preacher placed his hand on the man's shoulder and spoke with him briefly, then returned, smiling.

"My friend Charlie," he said, sitting down. As he sat, the student spied a thin black cushion on the bench beneath him.

"Hey that's cheating!" the student exclaimed. "You bring a cushion? And here I am, getting a sore butt every week."

The preacher laughed. "Sorry, my friend—privileges of the aged."

The student looked back at the man feeding the pigeons. "How do you know Charlie?"

A knowing smile spread across the preacher's face. "He comes to the food bank, and we've had some interesting conversations. He's been promising me he'll come to church, so I took the opportunity to remind him of his promise." The preacher's smile faded. "Actually, I wanted to see how he was doing, because he hasn't been looking so well and…" He glanced in

Charlie's direction, growing thoughtful. "Well, things can change quickly for guys like him."

The young man looked at Charlie, then back at the preacher. It occurred to him there was much he didn't know about this kind-faced preacher. For the first time, it struck him that this preacher had a life of his own—a family, perhaps, and friends. It seemed odd the thought hadn't occurred to him before.

After a few moments, the preacher turned to him and asked, "So, what were we talking about a minute ago?"

"I think you were about to discuss the next assumption."

"That's right." The preacher clasped his hands and looked into the young man's eyes. "Our next assumption is that a true revelation from God would be deeply transformational."

"Transformational? In what sense?"

"I think if a person arrived at an understanding of their purpose, it would transform them in profound ways."

That makes sense, the student thought.

"The most profound truth anyone can stumble across is their reason for being," the preacher continued. "Practically speaking, a person who discovered their purpose could begin to live accordingly. Imagine the sense of fulfillment they would experience."

"I guess I agree. You would finally be living as you were meant to live."

"Exactly," the preacher affirmed. "Which means you would expect the world's *true* religion to be distinguished from the others by evidence of positive transformational change in the lives of those who embraced it." The preacher's eyes drifted back in the direction of his friend only to find Charlie gone, and the pigeons wandering elsewhere in search of food.

Meanwhile, the student's thoughts had turned to some disturbing news he'd heard from a university friend. It turned out one of their mutual profs had been seen smoking a joint with some of the students in his class after-hours. *So much for the benefits of higher learning*, he thought cynically.

"Funny you should say that," the student deadpanned.

"What do you mean?"

"Nothing, really. Just that I agree. Truth should enlighten people." He paused. "But wouldn't members of any religious group—or denomination, or whatever—say they have been changed in some profound way by what they believe? I mean, isn't that the very point of religion?"

"I suppose so," the preacher replied. "But I think we could expect the 'true' religion ought to be marked by more evidence than the others. Evidence that's recognizable. I mean, think about it—if there were a group of human beings on earth who were truly living out their God-given purpose, shouldn't some evidence of it be clear?"

"I imagine so... but if it was so clear, why don't we already know who they are?"

"Good question," the preacher replied. "You're assuming, of course, that we don't know, and I'm not sure that's true. But if it's not evident to people, I think there's only one possible reason: some people don't want to know."

The student looked surprised. "Are you saying people wouldn't want to recognize the truth?"

"Well, what about moral responsibility?" the preacher suggested.

"What do you mean?"

"Knowledge of the truth should affect the choices we make, how we live our lives. Wouldn't that be incentive for some people to remain in willful ignorance?"

The student thought for a moment. "I don't know. It depends on the person, I suppose."

"In any case," the preacher added, "the point is, true religion ought to transform people's lives for the good—nothing less."

"And you believe Christianity transforms lives."

"I do," the preacher replied. "But perhaps I should ask you a question: has a follower of any religion apart from Christianity ever shared with you how their faith transformed their life in a profound way? Perhaps by helping them to love others better, break free from an addition, or cast off an immoral lifestyle?"

The preacher let the question hang, knowing the student wouldn't be able to quickly respond.

"I don't know, I'd have to think about it..." The student tried to call to mind what he knew about people of other religions. He had several friends who were Muslims. He also knew Hindus and Jews. Some seemed enthusiastic about their faith, claiming they found a source of comfort in prayer. Others appeared indifferent. One of his "spiritual" friends, who adhered to no religion at all, often related how she experienced a sense of peace through meditation. But none of them had ever made those kinds of claims, at least not that he could recall.

"I can't think of any at the moment," he replied finally.

"Fair enough. Now, have you ever heard Christians testify to those kinds of life changes?"

The question was a painful one. He had a cousin who had become a born-again Christian a few years ago, to the shock and horror of everyone in his family. His cousin had been a kind of bad boy until he found religion and quit his lifestyle of partying and drugs. There was no denying that he was *nicer*, but he also preached incessantly about his newfound faith and how his life was altered. Frankly, he found his cousin obnoxious and avoided him as much as possible…

He glanced over at the preacher, fearing irrationally that the preacher could hear his thoughts. The preacher waited with arms crossed.

Apart from his cousin, he knew about testimonies of Christians whose lives had been transformed. They were proverbial; the cable stations were full of them. Apart from his cousin, though, he had experienced little contact with Christians. He relayed the substance of his thoughts—minus his feelings about his cousin—to the preacher.

"And *I* can tell you," the preacher added, "of many individuals in our own church whose lives have been transformed in powerful and tangible ways. I bet nearly every church in the city could tell you the same thing."

The student looked mildly surprised. "But that's just speculation."

"Partly," the preacher affirmed, "but I have good reason to speculate. I know many pastors in our city and the kinds of things that happen in their churches. I know you would probably regard me as biased—and you would be right, by the way—but you don't have to take my word for it. You could talk to pastors and Christians from churches around the city and ask for yourself."

The student seemed to wince at the directness of the challenge. "I could also visit mosques and Buddhist temples and ask the same thing," he fired back.

"Absolutely, if you wish. But if your personal experience to this point is any indication, I doubt you would find the same kinds of testimonies there."

"So you think all these other religious groups are phonies?" The student's tone turned indignant.

The preacher's eyes widened. "No, not at all. I think many— probably most—are sincere. It's just that all religions can't be right, and the true religion *ought* to demonstrate a unique power to transform lives. I'm not trying to make Christians seem special or put down people of other faiths. But Jesus once said that 'wisdom is proven right by all her children.' What he was saying is that true wisdom is recognized by the results it produces—in this case, in the lives of people."

"But what about my friend, who says she finds peace through meditation? Doesn't that count?"

"I'm not saying it doesn't count, but I purposely made reference to tangible, lifealtering changes—like an ability to love others better, or shedding an immoral lifestyle— because changes related only to our *feelings* are subjective. I think you'll find most religious people will describe feeling greater inner peace, tranquillity, or being more spiritual or in tune with God when they practice their religion. But notice how subjective those things are."

The preacher's mouth felt dry, so he paused to sip his coffee.

This stuff is strong, he thought. *No wonder Starbucks is filled with students at exam time.*

"I feel a sense of peace when I spend time in the outdoors. I feel happier when I work out," the preacher continued. "But those experiences aren't evidence of knowing *truth*. The kind of subjective terminology that usually accompanies discussions about religion suggests that people's religious practices may help in some way or make them feel better. But we would expect more far-reaching change to occur in the lives of people who have discovered their purpose. And if you were to research it for yourself, I think you would discover that those are precisely the kinds of changes that have characterized the lives of Christians throughout history."

The student considered the implications. If what the preacher was saying was fact, Christianity certainly had some powerful evidence to recommend it.

"So you think those who practice other religions are sincere, just wrong,' the student said.

"That's right."

"But who are you to say what's true and what's not? Can't the beliefs of others be true for them?"

The preacher was surprised by the question. "Well, that's like saying the earth was flat because a long time ago people thought it was."

"What do you mean?"

"The earth was *never* flat. Believing that it was didn't change the truth. It sounds like you believe truth is subjective."

The student shrugged. "Why couldn't it be?"

"Because it defies common sense." The preacher tried to think of a relevant illustration. "Take gravity, for instance. A man who jumps out of a tenth-floor window can *believe* he can fly, but that doesn't make it so. To say his ability to defy gravity is 'true for him' would be silly. He's going to experience the truth—in this case, the truth of gravity—whether he believes it or not. The truth about gravity, like every other truth, has an objective reality that cares nothing for what people believe."

"Are you saying truth and reality are the same thing?"

"Well, the Greek word used for truth in the Bible means 'the reality lying behind an appearance.' I think that's a great definition. In the case of the world being round, for instance, the world may *appear* flat, but the reality—or truth—*behind* the appearance is that it's round. What that tells us is that we may perceive reality or truth in different ways, but that doesn't change or determine reality itself."

The student shrugged. "I'm not sold on truth being subjective. But it seems kind of arrogant to claim that what you believe is true and what others believe is false. That's one of the things people dislike about Christians—they aren't tolerant toward other people's beliefs."

"Well, I guess that depends on what you mean by tolerant," the preacher replied. "Christians don't condone violence or mistreatment toward people of other faiths. In fact, one of Christianity's main teachings is to love your enemies. But let me ask you, is it arrogant to claim that the earth is round even if some believe it's flat?"

"I suppose not."

"Right, because truth isn't an issue of ego. It's not about respecting—or disrespecting—people's beliefs. Respect has to do with our attitude, how we treat people who believe differently. We need to have the courage to be honest enough to recognize truth and admit falsehood. Simple logic dictates that all the religions of the world can't be right! Anyone who believes they've found the truth about God *ought* to reject conflicting viewpoints. That's not arrogance; it's good sense.

"In fact," he added, "I would suggest that the willingness of people from some religions to accept the 'truth' of other religions is actually evidence that what they believe *isn't* true. Hinduism is a good example. Hinduism is very accepting of other religious systems because it claims all religions present the same truth from a particular cultural standpoint. I believe Hinduism is a poor candidate for truth precisely because it accepts a wide spectrum of viewpoints that are in direct conflict with Hinduism—and each other."

The student looked uncertain.

"Just think about it," the preacher continued. "If God revealed the truth to humanity, would he really want those who know the truth to accept and endorse systems of belief that run *contrary* to the truth? It seems to me that Christians do what you would expect those who have the truth to do: proclaim it with passion and refuse all contradictory claims."

The student mulled over the preacher's logic. The fact that he couldn't disagree conflicted with the irritation he felt. Somehow it still seemed preposterous for any person or religion to assert that what they believed was truth and what others believed was a lie. Yet another part of him recognized that it was precisely the ability to discern truth from falsehood that he longed for. He decided that it was probably best to concede the point—for now.

"I guess that makes sense," he replied at last. "If you believe what you possess is the truth, you ought to reject everything else. The hard part is figuring out what the truth is."

The preacher nodded. The two figures sat in silence, aware of how wearying their discussion had been. They had covered a lot of ground, and once again the preacher had neglected his lunch. It seemed their conversation had reached a natural conclusion and their minds were too full to continue.

The plaza was nearly empty. The office workers who had come for lunch had returned to their air-conditioned cubicles and a handful of city workers in white uniforms, brooms in hand, had begun to troll the pavement for trash.

"Well, young man," the preacher said after a long breath. "I think we should call it quits for today. You game for another round?"

The student nodded. "Sure."

When they stood, the student surveyed the preacher. He hadn't realized how tall the preacher was. When they were sitting, they conversed eye-to-eye and their height difference wasn't noticeable, but standing side-by-side, the preacher was easily six inches taller. The young man felt dwarfed, and at the same time strangely comforted by the preacher's towering presence.

The preacher held out his hand.

As the student took it, he found the preacher looking down at him, his eyes conveying appreciation and respect. He couldn't help but smile. He had never conversed with another man and felt such a sense of equality and acceptance. Warmed by the affirmation, he began the short walk home.

CHAPTER FIVE:
Reverberations

The following Friday, the preacher arrived early, having learned that if he didn't eat before the student arrived, he was likely to go hungry. A group of young children ran around the plaza fountain, their shrill cries and laughter reverberating off the pavement.

The preacher watched them with quiet delight. He loved to people-watch, perhaps because he'd felt like an outsider as a kid, being skinny and awkward and the subject of much teasing. It had been easier to watch life happen from a distance than to risk entering in. Even now, despite the fact that he had learned to connect with people and enjoyed socializing, he still preferred to stand on the sidelines and observe in silence.

As his eyes swept the plaza, his thoughts turned to the student. He realized he was beginning to deeply look forward to these conversations, and that his affection for the young man had been steadily growing. In some ways, he reminded the preacher of a younger version of himself. Although most who met him in his role as pastor had difficulty imagining it, he had once been far from God and a fierce opponent of religion. But as with the young man, he'd possessed an increasing and sincere desire for truth.

"Alright, I'm here. Let's get started."

The student's sudden appearance and abrupt greeting once again startled the preacher. He wondered if the young man took pleasure in scaring him out of his wits each week.

"Oh, sorry about that," the student chuckled, seeing the preacher start. "I'm not very good at hellos—or small talk." He plopped down on the bench. He wore a white T-shirt with a yellow smiley face in the middle. The smiley face had a bullet-hole in it with a stream of red blood oozing out. The eyes were marked by two X's. The edges of an indistinct tattoo were just visible above the V of his collar.

"No worries," the preacher replied, smiling. "Just let me catch my breath." He placed his hand on his chest dramatically.

"So, where did we end off last time?"

"I think we were talking about being willing to stand up for truth. But I'm not sure what our last assumption was."

"I remember," the student replied. "The truth about God ought to change people."

"That's right.

"And you believe Christians show the best evidence of change."

"Did I say that?"

"Something like that."

"Yeah, I guess that's basically what I said," the preacher acknowledged. "But I'm less concerned about making the case for Christianity than I am about encouraging you to ask that question for yourself."

"Right, I gathered that. You haven't been too pushy—yet."

"Good."

Nearby, a rollerblader weaving his way through the throng of people suddenly wiped out, skidding painfully across the pavement.

"Ouch." Smiling faintly, the student seemed amused.

The rollerblader slowly stood. Both of his legs had skinned, bloody patches.

I'm glad those days are over for me, the preacher thought. If he were to fall like that at his age, he would probably break a leg—or worse.

"I think our next assumption goes along the same lines as the last," the preacher said, returning to the subject at hand. "The truth about God would change the world for good."

"Alright, unpack that one for me."

"There are two ways to look at it," the preacher began. "First, if God is good, you could expect His revelation to mankind to be beneficial. In other words, it should increase rather than decrease the amount of good in the world."

The student considered the argument. "I guess I would buy that."

"Okay. And second, true personal transformation will inevitably bring about transformation on a larger scale. As individuals are enlightened, their light will make a difference in the world at large."

The student nodded. "I think that's reasonable. But hasn't religion been a pretty mixed bag? I mean, religion may have brought some good to the world, but what about all the wars started in the name of religion?"

"That's true. But remember, we're not talking about religion *in general.* Simple logic tells us that the world is full of *false* religions, so it shouldn't surprise us that religion has caused some major problems in the world. What we're looking for is a religion that's had a powerful impact for good."

"And it's between Islam, Christianity, and—did we rule out Hinduism?"

"Not necessarily," the preacher replied. "They're still the most likely candidates. I did mention last time that Hinduism, for logical reasons, seems a more unlikely candidate than the other two. And to reiterate, our argument isn't airtight. We've conceded that it's possible the truth lies with another religion altogether; we're just trying to discern where best to start looking. The question for the moment is, which of these three religions appears to have most impacted the world for good?"

The student hesitated. This wasn't something he had thought much about before.

"I'm not sure."

"Okay, let's look at them one at a time. How has Hinduism— or Hindus as a group—been a force for good in the world? What comes to mind?"

The student thought for a moment. "I know some Hindus who are really nice people, very hospitable…"

The preacher nodded. "Me too. I've met some wonderful Hindus. But think global impact. Any associations come to mind?"

The only thing that came to mind for the student was a name. "Well, there's Gandhi."

"Good, Gandhi was Hindu. Among other things, Gandhi brought about a peaceful revolution in India that eventually resulted in their independence. That's fair game. Anything else?"

"That's all I can think of. But I live in the west. There's probably a lot about Hinduism I don't know."

"Absolutely," the preacher replied. "At the same time, if Hinduism had such a profound impact on the world, don't you think something else would come to mind? Something even people like us should be aware of?"

The student shrugged. "Hard to say."

"Okay, fair enough. What about Islam?"

The student knew some very nice Muslims. He also knew some who weren't so nice. But if he was honest, he would be forced to admit that the main associations he had with Islam were negative: war, terrorism, unrest. There was also honour killings and poor treatment of women...

Not exactly promising, he thought. He was sure there was more to know and understand about Islam, but that was all he knew.

"I don't know. Most of what you hear on the news is pretty negative. But I don't really know a lot about Islam, or Muslims, so it's hard to make a judgment."

"I'm sure that's true," the preacher said. "But again, isn't it interesting that nothing comes immediately to mind? I think it's fair to ask: if Islam has been a powerful force for good in the world, shouldn't it be evident? And why so many negative associations? I'm not saying all the negative reports with regard to Islam are all there is to know. In point of fact, I know some very decent, peace-loving Muslims who have done tremendous good right here in this community, so we need to beware of stereotyping individuals of any faith. Besides, we're not talking about *people* so much as *impact*—the impact of Islam's belief system on the world. I'm simply pointing out that if Islam truly has been a force for good in the world at large, it seems difficult to see."

The student appeared unconvinced. "I see your point. But again, I think there's a lot we don't know."

"True. Still, I think it's a fair question to consider. Now, let's move on to Christianity."

"Alright."

"Well, let's ask the same question. In what way has Christianity impacted the world for good?"

To the student's surprise, a series of names and images came quickly to mind—Christian missionaries feeding the poor, the Salvation Army program which distributed food and clothing at the university, names like Mother Theresa and Martin Luther King Jr...

He looked up at the preacher, his eyes narrowing involuntarily. He was hesitant to share his thoughts, not wanting to justify the preacher's own bias in favour of Christianity.

"I think there are some ways, for sure," he finally said. "Like missionaries and feeding the poor and whatever. But we live in the western world, where Christianity has been the main religion for centuries, so the fact that I'm aware of some of the good things Christianity has done isn't surprising."

The preacher nodded. "That's very true. In fact, I don't think we *could* have a completely objective opinion about the impact of world religions. But then, no one living in any other part of the world would, either. Which means we're *all* going to have to make a decision based on incomplete evidence."

"I guess."

"But back to the point, when you thought about the impact of Christianity, some positive things came to mind?"

"Sure."

The preacher could see the young man wasn't going to offer anything further. "I notice you mentioned the term 'missionary' when giving examples of Christianity's impact on the world. Did you know that the concept of a missionary—and missionary work—is Christian in origin?"

"I… I don't know. I've never really thought about it." The student looked puzzled. "Are you saying that people from other religions aren't taught to feed the poor or help people in need?"

"No," the preacher replied. "I'm simply pointing out that the sense of obligation we feel to reach out to the poor and destitute in remote areas of the world has its origin in the activities of the earliest Christians, who were given a mission by Christ to spread the message of God's love and forgiveness to the world, and to demonstrate it through their actions. Which they did, and which Christians continue to do up to the present day."

The student shrugged. "That may be true, but there are lots of organizations that help the poor and the sick that aren't Christian."

"That's true," the preacher replied. "But the fact that there are so many secular charitable and mission-oriented groups in the west today simply demonstrates how influential the teachings of Christ and the values of Christianity have been in western culture—even among those who claim to oppose the Christian message. And we haven't even touched on the positive contributions of Christianity in the areas of social justice, political reform, economics, literature, science…"

"Science?" the student interjected. "You're joking, right?"

"Not at all."

The student looked amused. "You're saying Christianity has made positive contributions to *science*?"

"I can't believe you're unaware of the scientific contributions of men like Keplar, Copernicus, Mendel, Pasteur…"

"Of course I am."

"They were all Christians, motivated by their Christian conception of the universe to undertake the study of it. In fact, science as we know it today owes its origins to devout Christian men who believed the physical world was intelligible, and thus worthy of study, because it was the product of an infinitely wise intellect."

The student looked surprised. "But isn't science now the archenemy of religion?"

The preacher shrugged. "Some people think so, but clearly some of history's greatest minds didn't see the two as incompatible. In any case, if God exists, in the long haul science should provide us with increasing evidence of that fact. I'm not a betting man, but I might be tempted to wager on that one."

The student couldn't help but smile at the aging preacher, who was clearly enjoying his philosophical musings on science and religion. He had to admit he knew very little about the Christian origins of science. He did know that Gregor Mendel was a monk, having learned that fact in high school chemistry, although he hadn't connected the dots to Christianity. And why should he? For most of his life, religion had seemed about as relevant to life as the fact that the moon had craters…

Bzzzzzzzzz.

He slid his cell phone out of his pocket. His mother's face appeared. She had texted him, saying she felt sick and needed him to come home right away. He sighed. He knew her well enough not to take her "urgent" messages too seriously.

Still, she may have run out of medication, and *that* was not a good thing...

"I'm going to have to get going," he said without looking up.

"Sure. Is everything alright?"

"Yeah, my mom just needs me for something."

The preacher saw that the young man had grown sullen. He shook the preacher's hand without making eye contact and started walking across the plaza, his hands in his pockets and his eyes downcast. As he watched the young man walk away, he wondered about the young man's family. He hadn't mentioned any siblings and he wondered if, like so many young men his age, he lived in the shadow of an absent father.

Feeling somewhat sullen himself, the preacher collected his things and strode off in the direction of the church.

CHAPTER SIX:
Lepers

As he neared the plaza the following Friday, the student passed a haggard-looking man seated on the sidewalk with his back against the stone facade of an office building. He was dark-skinned and dressed in a dirty denim jacket and khaki pants. His outstretched arm held a cup. A felt cap was pulled down over his eyes. The young man couldn't tell if he was resting or asleep.

As he passed, he remembered Charlie, the man he'd seen feeding pigeons by the fountain. The preacher's concerned words came to mind: *Things can change quickly for guys like him.* He reached into his pocket. He normally didn't carry cash, and was surprised to find some change wedged in the corner of his pocket.

Quickly and somewhat awkwardly, he approached the figure with his hand outstretched. The man remained motionless. Not wanting to draw attention to himself, or awaken the man if he had dozed off, he dropped a few coins into the man's cup. As he did so, he heard a wet *plunk*.

Horrified, he backed up.

"Hey!" the figure exclaimed. "What are you doing? That's my coffee, man!" He lifted the brim of his hat and sat up, his well-lined face screwed up in disgust.

"Sorry, I thought… I didn't realize…"

"Geez!" The man stood, walked over to a nearby trash can, and tossed his cup into it—coins and all.

Mortified at his mistake and eager to make a hasty exit, the student turned and hurried away, his face red.

Figures, he thought cynically. He wasn't accustomed to paying much attention to the many street people he passed in his travels each day; they were as much fixtures of the city as the flower boxes and the lampposts lining the downtown streets. But his weeks of conversation with the preacher seemed to alter his perspective. He was noticing things he hadn't noticed before.

And it wasn't just the poor. This morning, he had spied his mother standing in the kitchen, smoothing the edges of her work smock with a faraway expression on her face. He'd paused at the front door, transfixed. She looked so vulnerable and innocent. Young, almost. He found himself wondering what she had been like as a girl, not yet afraid.

As he spied the familiar form of the preacher through the throng of people across the plaza, he allowed himself a chuckle over his mishap with the unsuspecting "panhandler." Unlike the preacher, being a do-gooder seemed a poor fit for him…

"Good afternoon!" The preacher smiled as the young man approached. He slid over to make room on the bench. "How have you been?"

"Oh, alright," the student replied, not wanting to mention his embarrassing encounter.

"Glad to hear it. Did you eat lunch yet?"

"No. I don't usually eat lunch."

"Well, I was going to offer to buy you a falafel, if you're interested." He nodded in the direction of the Chip Truck parked in its usual spot on the east side of the plaza. Far away though it was, the aroma of grease was clearly discernible.

"Josef has the best in the city..."

"No thanks, I'll pass."

The two figures sat in silence for a moment, distracted by the strangely comforting noise of the city.

"So what's on the menu today, intellectually speaking?" the student asked.

The preacher's expression turned thoughtful. "Well, let's see, where were we? We've talked about transformation and world impact..." He paused. "There are a handful of assumptions left. They don't fall in any particular order. We can start with this one: a true revelation from God would be confirmed by supernatural evidence."

"Supernatural evidence?" The idea was intriguing. "You mean miracles? Like the parting of the Red Sea, that sort of thing?"

The preacher nodded. "More or less. It makes sense to believe God would manifest Himself in unique ways within the context of the 'true' religion."

"So, only in the lives of Christians or Muslims or whoever? You mean you don't think He would be active in the lives of other people?"

"What I mean is that He would act in a *unique way* in the lives of those who know and follow the truth."

The student shrugged. "But does 'unique ways' necessarily include miracles or the supernatural? I mean, what if nature is God's way of interacting with us?"

"Actually, I believe nature *is* one of the ways God interacts with us," the preacher affirmed. "But most religions believe God can and does act *super*naturally—in ways that defy or supersede the laws of nature." He paused in thought. "And I think that's a reasonable expectation. I also think God would want to provide confirming evidence of the truth and where He is most actively at work."

"You're saying that miracles would confirm which religion has the truth."

"Not exactly. I'm saying it makes sense to believe God would be *most active* within the context of the truth He gave. If the supernatural does occur—if miracles really do happen—I think we could expect them to happen with the most regularity within the context of the 'true' religion. So the question is, which religion demonstrates the best evidence of miracles?"

Not able to pass up the opportunity to jab the preacher, the student grinned. "Gee, let me guess…"

The preacher looked confused for a moment, then recognized the joke. "You're mocking me."

"Only mildly."

"Well, what do *you* think?"

The student shrugged. "Frankly, I don't have a clue. I've never seen a miracle and I don't think I know anyone who has."

"Fair enough. But I think there may be something to be learned just by examining the claims of the religions themselves."

"How so?"

"Well, which of the three religions we're looking at makes *claims* about miracles?"

"I know the Bible does. I don't know enough about the others to answer that."

"Okay, I'll help you out with this one." The preacher winked. The student looked back at him with a blank expression, so he assumed a more business-like tone. "Miracles are *most* central to the Christian faith. Islam accepts the concept of miraculous signs, but its founder, Mohammed, made no claims to have performed miracles. As a whole, Islam isn't characterized by claims about the supernatural…" The preacher shook his head. "Actually, that's not entirely true. Islam does recognize one important miracle: the divine inspiration and reception of the Koran by Mohammed. But apart from the Koran, Islam doesn't put much emphasis on the miraculous, generally speaking. Hindus believe that many holy men possess magical powers as a result of their spiritual devotion."

"Okay, so all of them make some claims about miracles. But how are we supposed to know whether any of their claims are true?"

"Well, if we're talking about proof, we may hit a dead-end— at this point, anyway. Let's just make some observations. The Koran excepted, Islam doesn't claim much evidence of miracles, although it does acknowledge such events in the lives of certain prophets, like Moses, Abraham, Elijah, and so on—prior to the founding of Islam."

"Wait a second," the student interjected. "Aren't those people in the Bible?"

"They are. Muslims share a belief in some of the same figures that appear in both the Jewish and Christian Scriptures."

"Why is that?"

"Well, it's a little complicated. In short, Islam affirms the divine inspiration of portions of the Jewish and Christian Scriptures."

The student looked perplexed. "But how can that be when their beliefs seem so different?"

"You would have to ask a Muslim about that. Theologically, I don't believe the Koran and the Bible can be reconciled, but one of the ways some Muslims explain the contradiction is by asserting the Bible has been corrupted and contains serious errors."

"Which goes against what we talked about earlier, right? That God would be able to preserve..." He paused, wanting to get the wording right, "the revelation of his purpose."

"Exactly right. Islam often presents itself as a kind of updated or corrected revelation, implying that earlier revelations were somehow corrupted. I think that constitutes a strike against it."

"That's true. But my point is that Islam, as a religion, doesn't depend on the presence of ongoing miracles, so it's not surprising they don't claim much evidence of the supernatural."

A moment passed while the student digested the thought. They were covering a lot of ground in a short time.

"But don't Muslims claim to see God as the reason behind a lot of events that occur in the world and in their lives?" He recalled hearing some of his Muslims friends refer to the outcome of political events, and even their education, as the will of Allah. "Wouldn't they see that as a form of supernatural intervention?"

"You're probably right. I believe God is behind a lot of the events that happen in the world and in the lives of people. But that kind of miracle is hard to ascertain—at least from an intellectual point of view. What we're looking for is credible evidence of the supernatural, something beyond the scope of ordinary events and the laws of nature."

"But who's to say that God even works that way? I mean, what if He just directs people's lives in a way that we don't even recognize?"

"That's very possible and we aren't ruling that out," the preacher replied. "But remember, we decided that it makes sense to believe God would be most active in the lives of those who embrace the truth. Since belief in the supernatural is so widespread, if God is in the habit of superseding the laws of nature, He is likely to do so with the most *frequency* in the context of the true religion."

"So we're not saying miracles even happen."

"Right. We're just investigating the possibility. But the first issue of relevance to our discussion is which religions even claims evidence of miracles. In terms of our three best candidates, all of them do. But I think Christianity differs significantly from the others in terms of its relationship to miracles."

"How so?"

"For starters, it was *founded* on the basis of a miracle: the resurrection of Jesus Christ."

"But didn't you just say Islam was founded on a miracle as well—the Koran?"

"That's true. But I think there's a great difference in magnitude. Being a book, the Koran, like the Bible, could theoretically be produced without divine intervention. On the other hand, the resurrection of someone from the dead isn't naturally possible and could only be explained in miraculous terms."

The student shrugged. "But all kinds of people are revived after they die today. Why does the idea of someone coming back from the dead need to be seen as a miracle?"

"The Bible's depiction of Jesus' resurrection is something entirely different from what you're talking about. Jesus wasn't merely revived. We know from the Scriptures that He was dead for a minimum of thirty-six hours. Then, after disappearing from the tomb in which He was laid, He appeared to his disciples in a new body. Jesus wasn't merely resuscitated; He was raised to a new life. Consequently, His resurrection was seen not only as a confirmation of His message, but of the truth of an afterlife for all believers."

The student looked mildly surprised. He'd never heard the resurrection explained in such detail. "So Christianity wouldn't exist without a belief in the resurrection?"

"Not *true* Christianity. It's one of the astounding facts about Christianity—that the very existence of the Christian faith depends upon the resurrection of Jesus being an actual historical event."

"But even if it was proven that the resurrection didn't happen, wouldn't people still follow Jesus?"

The preacher considered the student's question. It was an insightful one. The absence of a miracle certainly didn't rule out the emergence of a religion or the possibility of followers. History certainly demonstrated that religions could arise from something as ordinary as a wise man and his teaching.

"You may be right," he replied after a moment. "But it certainly wouldn't be the Christianity we know today. In fact, one of the most important figures in early Christianity, the Apostle Paul, who penned a significant portion of the New Testament of the Bible, said very plainly that if the resurrection of Jesus didn't occur, there was no basis for the Christian faith."

"I still don't see why that's the case."

"For early Christians, the miracle of the resurrection was proof that Jesus was divine. *Without* that event, they never would have known for certain if He was just a wise teacher or if He was who He claimed to be—the Son of God. When you think about it, despite being people of faith, the earliest Christians were pragmatists who recognized the value of evidence. Jesus made some powerful claims, and those claims needed to be validated in an equally powerful way."

"But doesn't that mean Christianity rests on a shaky foundation? After all, how can the resurrection be proven?"

"What it means, for certain, is that a claim of the supernatural lies at the heart of the Christian faith. And we've already concluded that we would expect evidence of the supernatural to be linked to a true revelation of God, so the claim is not absurd. Astounding, certainly, but not *illogical*."

"So the question is, did the resurrection really happen?

"Correct. And while that question poses some unique challenges, the Bible is clear that the early Christians had the proof they needed in the form a personal encounter with the resurrected Christ.' He paused. "There's actually a lot we could discuss about the subject, but right now we're trying to evaluate Christianity from a different angle. And there's more than just the resurrection to consider."

"Okay, go on."

"The Bible testifies that Jesus Himself performed miracles. Dozens of them are recorded in detail. Hundreds, perhaps even thousands, are alluded to."

"But that proves nothing."

"Except the point that the Bible depicts Jesus as a miracle-worker, undoubtedly the greatest *professed* miracle-worker in history. What's more, Jesus claimed that His miracles were evidence of the fact that He had been sent by God."

"But wouldn't leaders from other religions say the same thing? That their 'miracles' were proof they were sent by God?"

"Perhaps, but in the end it comes down to credibility. The interesting thing about Jesus' miracles, and what sets them apart from the kind of parlour-shop magic you often hear about in other religions, is that Jesus' miracles were almost always miracles of mercy."

"Like healing lepers," the student suggested.

"Right. Most involved healing the sick. He also supernaturally multiplied loaves and fishes to feed a hungry crowd, raised a widow's son from the dead, and so on."

The student grinned. "What about turning water into wine? It's pretty hard to see the compassion in that one."

"Aha! The miracle that everyone remembers about Jesus!" The preacher laughed. "Actually, you might be surprised to know that it was a miracle of mercy."

"Really?"

"The host at the wedding he was attending ran out of wine and Jesus' miracle of provision probably saved him from serious social embarrassment."

The student chuckled. "I never heard the story behind that one."

"Anyway, the point is, I think Jesus' miracles were unique in that they were exactly the *kind* of miracles you would expect to come from the hand of a loving and benevolent God interested in revealing Himself to the world. It's significant that Jesus *expressly claimed* that He had been sent by God to reveal the truth about God to humanity. And He claimed that His miracles were both evidence that God had sent Him and evidence of what God was like."

"Okay, I see that. But again, it's not proof."

"True enough. Here's an interesting fact to consider. Did you know that the historical references to Jesus we have *outside the Bible* don't attempt to deny that He was a miracle-worker?"

The student was taken aback. He wasn't even aware that there were any references to Jesus outside the Bible.

"No," he replied.

"It's true. And what it suggests is that Jesus' miracles were so numerous and well known that they were undeniable, even by those who didn't believe in Him."

The student had no firsthand knowledge of what the preacher was talking about. All he knew was that one of the arguments he'd encountered at university was that Jesus of Nazareth was probably a historical person who had been deified by His followers and whose life had been embellished with accounts of the miraculous. It was certainly something worth investigating further.

"What were you saying earlier about parlour tricks?" he asked after a moment. "I didn't get what you meant by that."

The preacher stretched. Beyond the plaza, the white edifice of the city's downtown casino flashed in the sunlight. "What I meant is that many of the so-called miracles you hear about within the context of certain religions—such as the ability of holy men to levitate, walk through fire, and so on—are things that tend to *astound* rather than point people to God. They're different from the miracles of Jesus in that they're primarily demonstrations of *power* that tend to draw attention and honour to the miracleworker rather than reveal the nature and intentions of God to people. Jesus' miracles had a very different character and effect. People were led to thank and praise God by the miracles of compassion Jesus performed. The Bible shows that Jesus wasn't interested in gaining notoriety or taking credit for miracles. He was always pointing people back to God."

The preacher paused. It was growing hot and his throat felt parched.

"On some occasions," he continued, "Jesus even led people away from the crowds so He could heal them in secret—which, of course, no one would do if they were out to impress people or draw a following. Jesus told people that He was doing God's work and God was the One they should thank—not Him. It seems to me that's the *kind* of miracleworker we would expect to be sent from God."

"That actually makes a lot of sense."

The preacher chuckled, surprised by the frank admission. "I'm glad you approve."

"No, I'm serious," the student repeated. "That's a really good point."

The student hadn't heard this perspective on Jesus and His miracles before. A part of him had been content to believe that Christianity, like other religions, was a fabrication intended as a way for religious leaders to assert authority over others. But he was suddenly struck by how incompatible the Bible's account of Jesus' miracles and conduct were with such a belief.

And if Jesus really could heal people, where did His ability come from? he wondered.

"Are you thirsty?" the preacher asked, interrupting his thoughts.

"Yeah, a little."

"I'll go grab us a couple of iced teas."

Before the young man could respond, the preacher stood and made his way across the busy plaza in the direction of the concession trucks. As he did, the student noticed, not for the first time, that he walked with an uneven gait. When he returned a few minutes later carrying two iced teas in paper cups, the student accepted the drink gratefully.

"There's one more thing," the preacher added as he sat down. "Christians throughout history and up to the present day claim to experience the same kind of miracles Jesus Himself performed."

The student's blank expression suddenly turned mischievous.

"What are you thinking?" the preacher asked.

"One word," the student replied. "Televangelists."

"Ah." The preacher leaned back, sipping his iced tea. "What about them?"

"Well, they're always making claims about miracles. But they're phonies."

The preacher shrugged. "Well, I don't know about that."

"Seriously!" the student replied, now agitated. "A few years ago, they even caught a guy who was claiming to hear things from God. It turned out he was being fed information about the audience through an earpiece."

It had been more than a few years ago, but like other nasty revelations about Christian leaders the story enjoyed an unnaturally long life in the media and in the minds of people.

"Fair enough," the preacher replied. He remembered hearing that same story in the news. It had been a sad indictment of Christianity in the eyes of many people, and he was grieved to hear of it. "There's no question there are phonies out there. But the fact that there *are* phonies just reinforces the point."

The student looked puzzled. "What point?"

"Well, phonies like that only exist because they're able to prey on the conviction among Christians that God *does* heal people."

"I get that. But so what? Aren't claims about miracles common in most religions?"

The preacher nodded. "I imagine, but with respect to the miracles within Christianity, there are couple of distinctions worth pointing out, related to their frequency and nature. Many Christians up to the present day claim to be recipients of miracles. In fact, in some circles miracles are regarded as regular occurrences. That speaks to frequency. Secondly, such miracles tend to be along the same lines as those Jesus Himself performed—miracles of healing and mercy."

"I'm not sure where you're going here."

"I'm pointing out that Christians are distinctive in that they have historically claimed to be the beneficiaries of a large number of miracles, which are benevolent in nature, and which they regard as evidence of God's activity among them."

"But we don't know if they're genuine or not."

A faint look of exasperation crossed the preacher's face. "As I've said, we're not trying to prove anything. We're just examining claims."

"I know, but aren't we going in circles?" The student was surprised by how quickly he could move from appreciation to scepticism. "We keep making speculations about things that could be entirely false. I don't know. Sometimes I just wonder if we're wasting our time."

The preacher sighed, unable to hide his own frustration. Perhaps the student was right. Perhaps they *were* wasting their time. The student's insistence on requiring proof—proof the preacher believed he would likely reject even if it were provided—was beginning to wear on him. In any case, he reasoned that they had gone as far as they were likely to go today. He noisily slurred up the dregs of his iced tea and placed the empty cup on the bench.

"Why don't we stop here for today?" he suggested.

The student was tired. He felt like he was drowning in his own thoughts. He took a deep breath and looked up at the angular forms of the office buildings surrounding them on every side. Sometimes the world seemed like such a large place, and he struggled to make any sense of it.

After a long silence, he spoke. "So, we'll continue next week?"

Despite his own misgivings, the preacher was pleased by the question. "Sure thing. Friday it is."

CHAPTER SEVEN:
Light-Bearers

As usual the preacher was the first to arrive. Stabs of pain raced up and down his spine as he sat. The hot, humid weather—usual for this time of year—meant his back was giving him more grief than usual. He considered taking a couple of Advil, which he always carried as a precaution, but decided against it. He was loathe to put chemicals in his body and took pain medication only as a last resort. As he struggled to find the most comfortable sitting position, the student arrived, circling around from behind the bench.

"Hey, Preacher!" The student smiled broadly, his hands behind his back. "I've got something for you." He stretched out his right hand. In it was a book.

The preacher instantly recognized the striking black and yellow motif on the cover.

"'The Bible For Idiots,'" he read. "Well, I'm not sure whether to be flattered that you thought of me... or offended about what you think of me."

"Your choice," the student retorted, clearly pleased with his joke. "I couldn't resist."

The preacher held the book at arm's length and pretended to study it. He sensed the book was the student's way of affirming their relationship after the tension of their last meeting.

"Well, I appreciate that. That was very thoughtful. I'm sure it will be a great source of help in ministering to my congregation."

"You're welcome." The student looked momentarily uncomfortable, as if unsure his words would be well-received. "So, are we moving to the next assumption?"

"Sure thing," the preacher reassured him. "I think we said all we need to say about miracles last time…" He put the book down beside him and winced noticeably with pain.

"Are you okay?"

"Yeah, my back's just a little sore today."

"Did you hurt it?"

"No, it's just an old injury that flares up from time to time." The preacher leaned back into a more comfortable position on the bench, folding his hands behind his head. He looked out over the sea of sweating pedestrians.

"Our next assumption concerns how we would identify a true messenger of God."

"A messenger of God? Are you talking about prophets?"

"I suppose," the preacher replied. "By a messenger, I mean the person—or persons—God would use to communicate His truth to humanity. Many of the world's religions have a main prophet or founder whom they believe received a revelation from God."

"Like Mohammed or Jesus."

"Exactly. And our assumption would be that a true messenger from God would reflect God's goodness."

"Reflect how?"

"For starters, I think we would expect their lives to have moral credibility."

The young man's face betrayed the hint of a smile. "And how would you define moral credibility?"

"That's a good question—and not an easy one to answer. I guess I would put it this way: if God is good, His spokesperson should reflect that. They should be moral, kind, benevolent, and so on. And if someone *claimed* to be a messenger from God but lacked those qualities—or demonstrated qualities that otherwise contradicted God's nature—I think we would have good reason to question their claim, as well as their message."

After pondering the preacher's statement, the student realized he had to concede the point. "I would agree with that."

"We would also expect their *message* to reflect God's nature," the preacher added.

The student nodded. "I would agree with that, too. But where does that leave us in terms of world religions?"

"Well, we've narrowed our focus to Islam, Christianity, and Hinduism, but Hinduism doesn't have a primary prophet, or even individuals we could recognize as divine revelators, so we'll have to put it aside for the moment." The preacher exhaled deeply. He was hot and could feel rivulets of sweat form under his golf shirt. "So, what do you know about Jesus and Mohammed?"

The student shrugged. "Not much, I know people from both religions would probably say they were good and holy men. I imagine the Koran and the Bible would confirm that. What else could you expect?"

"Let's stick to some things that could be easily discovered about each of them. For instance, I think one point of interest about their respective lives is that Jesus claimed to be sinless, while Mohammed did not."

"What do you mean by sinless?"

"Essentially, He was claiming that He'd never done anything wrong."

"In His entire life?"

"That's right."

The student was about to respond with his customary observation—that a claim wasn't proof of anything—but then thought better of it.

"So, Jesus claimed to be perfectly good?"

"Correct."

"That's quite a claim. Didn't He also claim to be God?"

"Yes," the preacher said. "He claimed to be God in the flesh. He claimed to be sinless. In fact, He claimed to be Truth itself, and the only Way to God! I think it's fair to say that Jesus made the most audacious claims of any person in history."

"But anyone could make claims like that."

"True, and they would be easily dismissed," the preacher replied. "But for some reason, the world hasn't been able to dismiss Jesus so easily."

"Clearly, and why do you think that is?"

"One of the primary reasons is His life and teaching. It would be very hard for even the staunchest non-believer to deny that Jesus is perhaps the most *moral* figure in all of human history."

"In all of history?" the student repeated. "Do you really believe that?"

"I do."

"But wouldn't Muslims say the same thing about Mohammed?"

"Perhaps. But in the end it comes down to how they lived and what they taught. In the case of Jesus and Mohammed, there are some clear differences. Consider how the two religions have spread, for instance. Historically, Islam spread through the advance of conquering Muslim armies, while Christianity spread through the preaching of Christ's message by His followers."

"So their approaches were completely different."

"Correct. And the reason their approaches were different harkens back to their founders—Mohammed and Christ. Muslim armies followed Mohammed's practice of conversion by the sword, whereas Christians followed Jesus' example of preaching the good news of God's forgiveness and appealing to people's consciences to turn from their sins. While Mohammed frequently fought the enemies of Islam, Christ forgave and prayed for those put Him to death and exhorted His followers to do the same." The preacher paused to let his words sink in. "And I think it's significant that more people have chosen to follow Christ *voluntarily* than follow the teachings of Mohammed and the Koran."

Pondering the preacher's words, the student made no reply.

"So the question before us," the preacher continued, "is which religious leader seems like a better candidate as a messenger of a benevolent God?"

The student sighed. Framed that way, the answer seemed too simple, almost absurdly clear. But there was something else—something about the preacher's depiction of the two faiths that seemed dishonest.

Suddenly his eyes were full of fire.

"Wait a second! What about the Crusades and the Inquisition and all of *that*? Christians killing Muslims and burning witches! What you said about Christianity being spread peacefully isn't true."

The preacher could see the student's objection was both passionate and valid. "Touché. It's true there have been some very dark periods in Christian history—and what I just shared was an oversimplification. It's true that Christians have at times employed violence and coercion, but I think those events differ significantly from the kinds of things you see within Islam."

"How so?" the student retorted. "War and violence seem to go hand in hand with religion. It's hard to believe God is involved in any of it!"

"I totally understand," the preacher replied. "But what human beings do and what God *wants* them to do may be very different things—even where there is true religion. I think the difference comes down to *consistency*."

"Consistency?"

"Yes. Consistency to the teachings of their founder," the preacher explained. "Christ rejected violence in relation to spreading His kingdom on the earth, so His followers are clearly in error when they resort to such means. However, history would suggest that Muslims who attempt to propagate their faith by violent means aren't acting outside the scope of Mohammed's own practice and teaching."

The student considered the preacher's statement. "But aren't there peaceful Muslims? Not all Muslims believe in violence."

"It's true that not all followers of either Christianity or Islam see things the same way within their own religion. But most of the different sects or denominations within each religion have one thing in common—their holy book. For Muslims, it's the Koran; for Christians, it's the Bible. Interpretations may differ, but the most objective way to evaluate each religion is to look at their source text."

The preacher interpreted the student's silence as permission to continue.

"The fact is, however they are interpreted, there *are* passages in the Koran where Muslims are commanded to kill, mistreat, or tax those who refuse to convert to Islam. So even if there are Muslims who believe such behaviour is wrong—and thankfully there are—it's easy to see why Islam continues to produce followers who teach and engage in such practices around the world."

"But aren't there passages in the Bible where God commands people to go to war and slaughter their enemies? I mean, isn't it all just a matter of interpretation?"

The preacher took a deep breath. "That's true, in a sense, although you won't find anything like that in the teaching of Christ. I suppose that ultimately the proof is in the pudding, in the kinds of societies each religion tends to produce." He shrugged. "In that respect, I think the facts may speak for themselves."

To the student, it seemed that people of different religions fought all the time—and although he knew that his conviction was vague and oversimplified, it was difficult to surrender.

"Let me ask you a question," the preacher said. "How many reports have you heard in your lifetime about Christians attacking Muslims—or any other religious group?"

Truthfully, he couldn't remember hearing any. In fact, it even *sounded* strange.

"I'll hazard a guess that you haven't," the preacher offered. "And that's because it's simply not reflective of Christian beliefs. Now, let me ask, have you ever heard news reports about Muslims persecuting or killing Christians or burning down Christian churches?"

The student thought for a moment. He had a vague recollection of reading an online article about Christian churches that were looted and destroyed by Muslims somewhere in Indonesia. Or was it Africa? He couldn't recall the details.

"I've heard of it happening," the student conceded.

"Right," the preacher continued. "Sadly, it's actually a pretty regular occurrence in many places of the world."

"And there's also terrorist attacks," the student added. Very slowly, he was beginning to see the distinctive differences between the two systems of belief.

"But isn't it only radical Islam that's to blame for that kind of stuff?"

"Perhaps," the preacher replied. "I'm just suggesting that there's a basis—a foundation—for what we know as 'radical Islam' within Islam itself which one would be hard-pressed to find within the teaching of Jesus."

The student looked at the preacher. He wasn't sure he agreed with the preacher's assessment, but it was clear after their many weeks together that the preacher was intimately familiar with the assumptions they'd been discussing.

"By the way," the student remarked after a moment, "I've never asked where you came up with these assumptions we've been talking about."

"They actually came out of my own search for God many years ago," the preacher replied.

The student looked surprised. "You mean you weren't always a Christian?"

"Hardly! Like someone else I know," he said, pausing for emphasis, "I was once a sceptical university student with a lot of questions."

It was difficult for the student to imagine that this kind-faced man hadn't always been a preacher.

"So, what were you like before you were a Christian?"

"That's quite a broad question," the preacher replied, as if to suggest he didn't realize what the student was driving at. "But if you're asking if I was a nice guy, the answer is no." His eyes drifted downward as memories of his younger self came to mind. "The truth is I was a very confused, selfish person who didn't know how to love people at all."

"Really? That's hard for me to imagine."

The student held the opinion that people were kind—or not—owing to their temperament. The idea that someone's nature could be dramatically altered was foreign and surprising.

"Well, I'll take that as a compliment." The preacher smiled weakly. "But I certainly can't take credit for the change. If I seem different from the person I once was, I can only attribute it to God's work in me."

"Right." The student shifted position, feeling suddenly uncomfortable. The sensation surprised him. They had been talking about God for almost an hour—and now for no apparent reason the mention of God made him uncomfortable. "So, these assumptions… were something you read about?"

The preacher shook his head. "Not really, although some of them were definitely born out of the books I was reading at the time. I guess they arose in my mind as I was considering the possibility of God's existence and of discovering the truth. I probably wouldn't have been able to articulate most of them at the time, but they more or less guided my search as I wrestled with the same dilemma we've been discussing—how to discover which religion is right."

The preacher glanced at his watch. He had a counselling appointment with a couple from his church in half an hour. The couple was new to the church and had a teenage daughter who'd just announced she was pregnant. As could be expected, her parents were struggling with a mixture of shock and anger; he wanted to have some time before their meeting to prepare and pray. The heat was also getting to him and he was uncharacteristically anxious to return to his air-conditioned office.

"I think we're going to have to wrap things up for today, my friend," the preacher announced. "I'd love to stay and chat a while longer, but I have to head back."

"Okay."

Looking at the young man, the preacher noticed that he didn't appear to be sweating at all. *Amazing youth*, he thought.

"So, are we on for next Friday?"

"Absolutely." The preacher stood, steadying himself with one hand on the bench.

The student jammed his hands into his pockets and shifted his feet self-consciously. "Thanks, by the way. I've never had an older person... I mean..." He blushed, realizing the indelicacy of his words. "No one's ever taken the time to talk with me the way you have. I just want to say I really appreciate it."

It was clear that it was difficult for the student to be so vulnerable with his feelings. As the preacher looked at the young man, a strong feeling of love welled up within him, and along with it the memory of another young man, slightly taller and more reed-like, with boyish good looks and deep blue eyes.

"Hey, we're in this together," the preacher replied. He offered his hand. "Believe me when I say the pleasure is mine." He shook the young man's hand, then turned away and began to weave his way through the crowded plaza.

As the student watched the preacher depart, he couldn't see that the preacher's eyes were welling up with tears.

CHAPTER EIGHT:
Kings and Beggars

The hot, muggy weather continued throughout the following week. On Friday morning, it began to rain and didn't let up until a little before noon. Both the preacher and the student found themselves wondering if the other would forgo their meeting.

The preacher was first to arrive. He spread a blanket across their customary bench and sat down. He waved at Josef, the owner of the Chip Truck across the plaza, who was just beginning to set up. The pavement was plastered with leaves and brightly coloured petals which the heavy rain had stripped from the trees and flowerbeds.

Petals on a wet, black bough, the preacher thought, recalling a line from a haiku he had studied many years ago.

He soon spied the young man enter the plaza from the street, looking wet and dishevelled.

"Wasn't sure you would be here," the student called out. As he drew nearer, the preacher saw that his jeans and T-shirt were soaked through.

"Did you walk?" the preacher asked, surprised.

The young man grinned, smoothing his wet locks. "I always walk," he replied. He looked down at the blanket. "Now, that's something I never would have thought of."

"Well, you can't help but remember certain things as you get older—like how uncomfortable it is to have a wet butt. Of course, there are also all the things you start to forget…"

The student laughed. "Well, I appreciate it, although I'm not sure it will do me much good at this point." He looked down at his soaked jeans and the dark patch that was already spreading out on the blanket beneath him.

"Probably not," the preacher mused. "Looks like I should have brought a towel instead."

"That's alright. The sun's starting to come out. I'm sure I'll dry off."

"So, how have you been?"

"Okay. Just discovering that I hate the courses I chose for summer session."

"What are you taking?"

"Adolescent Psychology and The History of Theater."

"That sounds like a pretty odd pairing."

The student looked mildly embarrassed. "Yeah, well, I'm still trying to discover what I'm interested in."

"I see."

"Sometimes I'm not even sure what I'm doing in school in the first place."

The preacher nodded. He had heard other young adults make similar statements about their studies over the years. He suspected the problem stemmed from a deeper lack of purpose which seemed to characterize the culture more and more. Curtailing his urge to wax philosophical on the subject, he decided to try to cheer the young man up.

"You're a bright young man. I'm sure you'll be successful, whatever path you choose."

The student gazed at the preacher, as if testing his sincerity. "In any case, I don't think I can afford to change my major again, that's for sure. Otherwise I'll be in school until I'm forty and it'll take me the rest of my life to pay off my student loans."

Overhead, the clouds broke and the sun flared down through the hazy air. Seeing that the rain had cleared up, people trickled back into the plaza.

The student stretched out his legs to catch as much of the sun's rays as possible, in the hope of drying his soaked jeans. He donned the pair of mirrored aviator glasses he had hooked on his jeans pocket.

"So, are we ready to pick up from where we left off last time?" the preacher offered.

"Sure. Shoot."

The preacher paused. The student looked back at him, his eyes completely hidden behind metallic lenses. The preacher always felt uneasy talking to people wearing sunglasses. There was something unnerving and impersonal about not being able to see a person's eyes when you talked with them. He found it irritating and vaguely disrespectful. Perhaps his way of thinking was antiquated.

"Concerning our next assumption," he continued, "I think it's reasonable to expect that the true religion would be inclusive."

"By inclusive, you mean accepting of everyone?" the student inquired.

"Not exactly." The preacher's reply drew a quizzical look. "I mean that the truth should be accessible to anyone, regardless of their ethnicity, gender, education, social and economic status—and any other circumstance of life that might distinguish one person from another."

"Isn't that the same as being accepting of everyone?"

"Well, I suppose it depends on what you mean by accepting. It makes sense to believe that God would accept people from every walk and circumstance of life, *provided* that they were willing to comply with what He requires of them."

The student recoiled. Compliance sounded suspiciously like mindless obedience.

"So, acceptance with conditions."

"Certainly," the preacher replied. "None of the things we mentioned—gender, ethnicity, social or economic status, and so on—should be a barrier to understanding and responding to the truth about God. At the same time, we need to recognize that not everyone would choose to accept and follow the *way* of truth. So, the true religion won't necessarily preach unconditional acceptance, but rather that all may come."

The student's apprehension lessened somewhat. "Okay, I see what you're driving at. The truth about God should be a message for 'everyman'; everyone should be able to get in on it."

"Exactly. So what we *wouldn't* expect is for the true religion to cater or be relevant only to a specific group of people. Nor should its message be so difficult to understand that only the very intelligent or the educated would get it. For people to be unable to understand or respond to the truth about God because of factors which are beyond their control would be unjust."

"Absolutely," the student replied enthusiastically. "I totally agree with that."

The preacher smiled. The issue of the universality and accessibility of truth was a matter of deep personal passion and he was delighted to find an answering passion in the young man.

"Now, in terms of our three current candidates, Hinduism is the least prolific, with the vast majority of Hindus residing in India. Islam and Christianity, on the other hand, have been embraced by very diverse groups of people in various parts of the world."

"So Islam and Christianity are the most prolific religions." The student smiled knowingly. "I sense there's a *but* coming…"

The preacher laughed. "You're right. But I think there are some interesting differences."

The student crossed his arms, still smiling broadly. "Naturally. Go on."

The preacher's face flushed as he felt a twinge of embarrassment at both his enthusiasm and predictability. His own beliefs were no secret, and he had no intention of feigning complete objectivity, but he began to wonder if his bias was colouring their discussion too deeply.

"Well, let me ask you, where are Muslim populations located throughout the world?"

The student thought for a moment. "In the Middle East. Africa. Parts of Asia, I think. I'm not sure where else."

"Right. Islam is concentrated primarily in Arab countries of the Middle East, North Africa, and some parts of Asia. What about Christianity?"

The student shrugged. "In the west—western Europe, North America."

The preacher nodded. "That was pretty accurate a hundred years ago. But you might be surprised to know that Christianity has now been embraced by large populations on every continent. In fact, countries like Russia, China, Brazil, and Nigeria have some of the largest Christian populations in the world."

The student had always thought of Christianity as a distinctly western phenomenon. It was intriguing to hear that this was not actually the case. "Okay, so why the difference?" he asked.

"The answer is complex," the preacher replied, "and I'm not qualified to answer it—except to point out that the difference may suggest that Christianity has a broader global appeal than Islam."

"Are you saying the reason it has broader appeal is because it's more inclusive than Islam?"

"Perhaps, but I was actually reasoning in reverse—that Christianity's global appeal likely speaks to the issue of its relevance to people from diverse backgrounds. In other words, although both religions essentially preach a message that says 'all may come', Christianity has clearly been more successful in drawing individuals from all people groups and walks of life."

"So, better evidence that its message is the truth."

"Potentially. At least in the terms of our assumption."

"But what if the reason is something different entirely—like economics?"

The preacher was intrigued. "What do you mean?"

"Well, let's face it. Christianity took root in the western world where much of the world's wealth is concentrated. Wouldn't it be easier for Christianity to spread, given the economic reach of western nations?"

"That's a good point—I hadn't thought of that. I'm sure economics *has* been a factor. Although that begs an interesting question: is prosperity the cause or the result of the spread of Christianity?"

The student shrugged. "I don't know enough about history to answer that. I'm just saying there's probably a connection."

"Fair enough." Recalling their previous conversation about Jesus and Mohammed, the preacher continued. "Do you remember a few weeks back, when we were talking about how Islam and Christianity have spread?"

"Sure," the student replied.

"We pointed out that Islam appears to have spread largely through military conquest and Christianity through peaceful proselytizing."

"Right, minus the Crusade and the Inquisition."

The preacher smiled. "Right, point taken. My point is, I think the way in which two religions spread may speak to the issue at hand."

"How so?"

"Well, if you were to look at a map, you would see that despite the fact that it's been around for somewhere in the neighbourhood of 1,400 years, geographically Islam has been largely limited to the nations that were conquered by Muslim armies in the years immediately following its founding. What does that suggest to you?"

"I don't know," the student said. "That it stopped spreading at some point, I guess. That its influence was limited by something. Maybe culture, or other existing religions."

The preacher nodded. "Perhaps. It may also suggest that Islam's expansion was largely connected to its military might, whereas Christianity would seem to owe its expansion to other factors—such as its message."

"I'm not sure I buy that. I mean, hasn't Christianity spread as a result of colonialism by western nations? I know from history class that wherever the Europeans went, they brought Christianity with them."

"That's an excellent point," the preacher replied. "I imagine the connection between conquest and religion is undeniable in both cases, but there's an important difference that shouldn't be overlooked—namely, that Muslim armies conquered territory with the express purpose of extending the reach of Islam, whereas the Christian nations of Europe acted for complex reasons, not primarily to extend the reach of Christianity."

"But what's the difference?" the student said. "Conquest is conquest, isn't it?"

"Perhaps. But consider that Christianity—historical exceptions aside—is *offered* to people, not forced upon them, even today. Many of those around the globe who call themselves Christian, myself included, weren't born in Christian families or forced to convert, but came to Christ willingly and voluntarily, drawn by His message, not through fear of reprisal or coercion. I'm not sure the same could be said about Islam." He paused, then decided to take another tack. "Have you ever been approached by a Christian who shared the message of Christ with you?"

The student thought for a moment. His cousin, of course, had initiated several uncomfortable conversations with him about his need for Christ over the years. He had also been approached by Christians on the street from time to time who wished to share their faith (he usually declined) or give him some literature. He glanced back at the preacher, once again struck by the irrational fear that the preacher could hear his thoughts.

"Sure," he responded after a moment.

The preacher nodded. "Right, and the reason is that Christians have a sense of mission about spreading the truth of God—not politically or militarily, but out of love."

Love? he thought. *Is it possible to love people you don't even know?*

At face value, the idea seemed absurd. He had his hands full just trying to love the people closest to him. He thought of his mother and his girlfriend. A vague sense of guilt washed over him.

"In fact, during the last century," the preacher added, "literally millions of people around the world have come to faith in Christ through the simple preaching of Christian missionaries who voluntarily travelled to foreign nations to spread Christ's message of God's love and forgiveness."

The preacher paused as a flood of images and emotions coursed through him. He was deeply committed to world missions as a matter of principle and privately hoped he would have the opportunity to preach the message of Christ abroad himself one day. His sense of urgency had been growing over the past few years as he became more acutely aware of his age and physical limitations.

Although it was impossible to tell with his sunglasses on, the student seemed to be thinking over the preacher's words.

"Right up to the present day," the preacher continued, "Christians have willingly sacrificed their lives in order to offer the message of Christ to those who needed to hear it, demonstrating that they would rather be killed than kill. I think that's exactly the kind of behaviour you would expect of people to whom the truth of God has been entrusted."

The student crossed his arms and leaned back. It was true. He had met people from various faiths, many of whom had been sincere. Some were extraordinarily nice, but apart from the Muslim group on campus that distributed leaflets about Islam from time to time, none had ever approached him with the express purpose of sharing their beliefs—apart from Christians. Not that he *minded*, of course. He normally had a strong aversion to people trying to sway him to their beliefs. The very fact that he had continued so long in his conversation with the preacher struck him as both extraordinary and out of character.

But this preacher was different. From behind his camouflaging sunglasses, he peered intently at the older man. The preacher was unlike any person—religious or otherwise—he had ever met. Kind, intelligent, open-minded, and clearly convinced of what he believed. He found himself wondering what Christians throughout history had been like. Had they been like this man? Were there other Christians in the world like him? Had Jesus been such a man?

The preacher leaned forward. It was becoming unbearably hot, and he would have to change his shirt back at the office; the one he wore was nearly soaked through with sweat. They had covered a lot of intellectual ground and the young man seemed to be absorbed in thought. Probably best that they called it a day.

He turned toward the student. "Well, my friend, shall we stop?"

Startled, the student sat up and rubbed his hands over his jeans. They were nearly dry—although his shoes were definitely another story.

"Yeah, sure. I'm looking forward to getting into some dry clothes."

"And I'm looking forward to my air-conditioned office," the preacher responded.

Agreeing to meet again the following Friday, the two shook hands and dissolved into the sea of people now crowding the steamy plaza. Overhead, a fighter jet passed low over the city, the deep roar of its engines swelling and then dissipating like low thunder.

CHAPTER NINE:
Fractures

When the preacher returned to the plaza the following Friday, he was surprised to find the student already waiting. He guessed from the young man's posture that he had been there for some time.

"Good morning," the preacher said warmly. "I think this is the first time you've beaten me."

"Yeah," the student replied. He seemed distracted, more sombre than usual.

"How are things?"

"Okay," he said without turning to look at the preacher. His eyes were focused on some faraway object. "Can I ask you a question?"

"Sure."

"What are you supposed to do when someone wants something from you that you don't have?"

The preacher paused, wondering at the source of the question. "Well, you can't give it. You can't give what you don't have."

"I know," the student responded slowly. "It sucks."

"Is this something you want to talk about?"

The student scowled, his face contorting with bitterness. "I don't know. My girlfriend wants me to love her, but I don't think I do. And I don't think I can."

"I see," the preacher replied. "Have you told her that?"

"No. She'd be devastated."

The preacher nodded. "Well, I imagine she'll be devastated sooner or later, you know. Women have a way of sensing these things."

"I know... I think she already knows, but I feel so helpless!" The young man's voice rose with anguish. "What am I supposed to do? I can't help the way I am! I want to love her, but I don't *feel* anything. And I don't know why—I *want* to. I don't know what's wrong with me."

"I understand."

The student looked at him with an equal mixture of surprise and disbelief. "You do?"

"Sure. I've been there myself, and I think everyone struggles with the same problem—to a greater or lesser degree. Love is a scarce commodity, and you can't give it if you don't have it."

"So I'm doomed."

"Well, perhaps."

The student smiled wryly. "Great. Thanks for the encouragement."

The preacher laughed. "Well, what I mean is, we're *all* doomed if we keep trying to look for the love we need in each other. All of our cups are nearly empty."

"I know mine is," the student admitted. "And it feels unfair that she wants something from me I don't feel capable of giving. But then when I think about it, I just get angry, because I know it's not wrong to want to be loved! I mean, I want the same thing. Who doesn't?"

"Everyone does. We all want a full cup—but draining what little others have doesn't really help anybody in the long run. Nobody winds up satisfied."

"So the world's messed up."

"It sure is."

Across the plaza, barely visible through the throng of pedestrians, a group of children were playing tag. One of them, a young girl in pigtails and a yellow dress, fell as she tried to tag her friend. Looking down at her skinned hands, she began to cry.

"But *why* is it so messed up?" the student continued. "I mean, if we're all wanting the same thing, what's our problem? Why do we want what we can't have?"

The preacher's expression turned thoughtful. Painful images flashed through his mind. "I thought the same thing when I was young. As a child, I remember seeing my relatives fight when we got together during the holidays, and it was *so strange*." His voice inflected with feeling. "I could sense how much everyone loved each other and loved being together, yet inevitably an argument would start over something silly... and it would just grow and grow until people were screaming at each other." The preacher shook his head. "It just seemed so insane. All I could think was, why can't we all just love each other? It seemed so simple—here was a roomful of people all wanting the same thing, yet somehow unwilling or unable to experience it."

"I know!" The student chuckled, exasperated. "Why is life like that?"

"Now *that* is a very good question. And I think the answer may relate to our discussion."

"How so?"

"I think that's something we could assume the truth about God should explain—what's wrong with the world, and why."

"Does the Bible answer that?"

"It does. Most religions have what we would call a world-view—a concept of the universe and how it works. All religions articulate a worldview—a concept of the universe and how it works. Many people subscribe to a worldview in which the universe and everything in it are a product of chance. According to that worldview, life really has no inherent meaning because the universe has no inherent purpose. Each worldview supplies different answers to the questions we choose to ask about the universe, our existence, and the details of our lives.

"But the relevant question, if we're looking for the truth, would be which worldview best explains the world in which we live? It's logical to assume that the worldview set forth by the true religion would be the one that best describes our human reality."

It was hard for the student to imagine religion contributing to a person's understanding of life. If anything, religion seemed to be the source of a lot of *un*reality, fables and fairy tales...

"You see, a worldview is just a concept of the universe. Now, if God revealed the truth about the universe to us, we would expect that truth—that worldview—to provide the best answers to our questions about life."

"Okay, so which one is it?"

The preacher laughed. "Since when was it my job to provide answers? I thought this was a discussion."

The student smiled weakly. "I know. But frankly I don't have much energy to argue today. I know you believe what the Bible says. I just want to know what that is."

"Alright, fair enough. The worldview set forth in the Bible begins with the world being created by God. It goes on to explain that the world was marred—messed up, to use your terminology—through man's sin."

"That's the Adam and Eve story, right?"

"That's right."

"But doesn't it make more sense to believe the story is allegorical and not literal? I mean, are we supposed to believe in a literal Garden of Eden and all of that?"

"Well, the Bible certainly treats the story literally. Even science seems to affirm that mankind is descended from a single woman." He paused to look levelly at the young man. "If God exists, is it really so outrageous to believe that some extraordinary events took place in the lives of the first two people?"

The student shrugged. "I don't know. But it's stories like that that make the Bible hard to believe—Adam and Eve, Noah and the flood—stories that seem too far out to be true or literal."

"But if there really is a God, a whole lot of extraordinary things suddenly come into the realm of possibility, don't you think? I mean, if God created mankind, why wouldn't He interact with them in extraordinary ways? Why wouldn't He record those events if they're relevant to the human condition? The kind of reasoning that dismisses those events as fabrications is the same reasoning that assumes the *non*-existence of God."

"So if God exists, stories like that could be true."

"Right."

The student sighed. Part of him desperately wanted to believe that what seemed incredible was possible.

"If God created the world, the supernatural isn't only possible, but probable," the preacher added. "What's called for in cases like this is a suspension of disbelief."

"Meaning?"

"It's a literary term. It suggests a willingness to put aside our tendency to disbelieve for the sake of entering into a story—or in our case, a discussion. Because if the Bible turns out to be a good candidate for the truth for various *other* reasons, we'll eventually be forced to consider the possibility that the supernatural events described in Scripture are also true."

The student smiled slyly. "If you eliminate what is impossible, then whatever remains—however unlikely—must be the truth."

The preacher was amused. "Arthur Conan Doyle."

"No, Spock. *Star Trek.*"

The preacher laughed. A boyhood fan of Sherlock Holmes, he knew the words were spoken by the eccentric detective in one of Doyle's final stories. For some reason, he enjoyed imagining them spoken by the stoic Vulcan. "I'm not sure that's exactly what I'm saying, but I like the quote."

"So for the moment we need to forget about how ridiculous some of the stories in the Bible seem."

"Right. What's interesting about the story of Adam and Eve is that it establishes what I think is a very important idea at the foundation of the Christian worldview."

"Which is?"

"Which is that the world is not what it should be because *we* are not what we should be."

The student's thoughts drifted back to his girlfriend. Last night's argument was still fresh in his mind. She had left in tears—again—after expressing doubts that she would ever be a priority in his life. He had watched her walk away with a sense of detachment. He knew there was something missing within him, but he seriously doubted the Bible could explain what it was.

"Because Adam and Eve sinned against God?" he asked after a moment. His question had a mocking tone.

"That's right." The preacher paused. "Most people recognize that frustration and disappointment is part of the human condition. But if human beings were merely accidents of nature, it would be odd that we should experience a longing for something we can't seem to attain, and a sense of disappointment in life and in ourselves."

"Couldn't that just be the product of the fact that life *has* no meaning and we wish that it did?"

"But if we're simply the products of random forces, why would that be the case?" the preacher asked. "It seems to me we would expect to find fulfillment in a survival-of-the-fittest scenario—since that's what formed us. But people who struggle to rise above others actually experience the opposite. They feel *less* fulfilled. The biblical worldview, on the other hand, provides a good reason for our struggle. It suggests that we've lost connection with God—and therefore our purpose—through sin, and *that* is the source of our frustration."

The student's eyes narrowed. "And how would you define sin?"

"The Bible defines sin in a number of ways. It means to miss the mark, to disobey God—"

"Well, why would it be wrong to disobey God? Did God create us to be robots? Why wouldn't He allow us to make our own choices?"

"The Bible says that He *does* allow us to make our own choices. But if we make bad choices, we can expect bad results."

"So God knows what's best, and we don't."

"It makes sense to believe that a benevolent God would know what's best for us. If He created us, He would certainly have the right to command us to do or not do certain things—just as parents have the right to do the same with their children…"

"Wait a second." The student felt agitated. "What you're saying is that God created us, then He *told* us what to do, and because we—or Adam and Eve, I guess—*chose to think for themselves*, we're now doomed to frustration?"

The preacher sighed. "Well, that's an oversimplification—"

"But that's basically what you're saying," the student cut in. "How can an intelligent person accept that? And what's the solution? Listen to everything God says and that will fix all our problems? That seems laughable."

The preacher paused. The student's objections weren't surprising. He wanted to answer them, but wasn't sure how best to proceed. He decided to take a different tack.

"Okay, let's back up and just look at the human condition itself."

He paused, waiting for some cue that the student was willing to follow. The student's arms were crossed and his expression was one of indignation, but he made no reply.

"I think everyone, if they're honest," the preacher continued, "recognizes that there's something wrong with the world."

"What if it *isn't* screwed up? What if we just don't like it?" The student wasn't prepared to abandon his line of reasoning too easily.

"Well, that might be true. But we certainly *experience* it as screwed up. Truth, if you recall, is about the reality lying behind the appearance—or, in this case, experience. Even on a practical level, is the world the way we want it to be or long for it to be? The very fact that we identify the pain and suffering in the world as problems that need to be *resolved* suggests that at a core level we recognize something is wrong. The Bible says this something is very close to home—it's *us*."

"So people are the problem?"

The preacher couldn't tell if the question was sincere or defiant. "How can we doubt that most of the problems we experience are the result of our own choices? People commit murder, start wars, oppress the poor, and pervert justice. There's clearly something wrong with us, and the Bible gives a credible explanation as to what's wrong."

"What if all that is just the nature of existence—the struggle for survival?"

"Well, it *could* be. Evolution can explain why the world is the way it is, but it doesn't provide a satisfying answer as to why we *feel* the way we do. Going back to my point, the Bible says that the world is messed up precisely because we have cut ourselves off from the Source of our life and become corrupt. We've turned from the path that would bring us peace—the path of love."

"I thought you said it was because we disobeyed God."

"I did. And God *is* love. Love is God's nature and the basis of all His commands."

"Are you serious?"

Once again, the preacher couldn't tell if the question was sincere or not. "Yes."

"Well, what about sex before marriage?" the student fired back. "The Bible says that's wrong, but why can't people have sex if they love each other?"

The preacher knew how he wanted to respond, but it was risky. He took a deep breath.

"Are you sleeping with your girlfriend?" he asked suddenly.

"Excuse me?"

"Your girlfriend, the one you were telling me about. Are you having sex with her?"

The student blushed and then laughed nervously, feeling a mixture of shock, indignation, and embarrassment. "I know you don't approve... but yes, I am."

"I thought you said you don't think you love her."

"Well, I don't know if I do or not. I don't think I do—but you don't *have* to love someone to have sex with them. We're adults. We can choose to have sex if we want."

"Certainly you can," the preacher said. "But in this case, sex is not an expression of love, correct?"

The student shrugged. "I guess that's true."

"But let's imagine for a moment you believed you *did* love her. Why do you think God would say sex before marriage is wrong—even if you believed you loved the person?"

"I don't think God said that. That's my point. I don't think it *is* wrong."

"Okay, fair enough. But have you given any thought as to why the Bible says that it's wrong?"

"I think it's just outdated thinking."

"Let me just give you some food for thought. Sex and reproduction are connected. Would you agree?"

"Of course."

"Throughout most of history, if a man had sex with a woman, there was a good likelihood that the woman would end up pregnant. Now, if the man and woman weren't married, and the woman became pregnant, their child would be born out of wedlock—provided they didn't get married afterward, correct?"

"Yeah, but I don't see your point." The student felt agitated at the simplicity of the preacher's questions. He didn't like being condescended to.

"Okay, stay with me here. Now which *child* do you suppose would be happier—a child with both parents married and living in the same home, or a child with one absent parent?"

"I think a child could be happy either way."

"That might be true, but I'm asking which child do you think would *likely* be happier."

"Probably the child with married parents."

"I would agree." The preacher paused. "Now which *woman* do you think would be happier—the woman with a husband helping her raise the child, or the woman with no husband? And keep in mind that many fathers in that situation choose to have no contact with the mother *or* child."

"I see where you're going with this," the student shot back. "But that was a whole different world than the one we live in today. There would have been practical benefits to keeping sex for marriage, for sure—which is probably why it's in the Bible. But that doesn't mean it's really an issue of right or wrong."

"Is the world really so different today? I mean, what's changed?"

"Well, birth control, for one thing! Sex doesn't automatically mean pregnancy anymore."

"Actually, it's never *automatically* meant pregnancy, just the possibility," the preacher said. "The real question is, is it *loving* to demand the pleasure of sex when it could very well produce a tragic situation for both mother and child—and we haven't even mentioned the repercussions for the father—"

"But as I said, birth control has changed all that."

"I disagree. All contraception has done is lower the probability of a pregnancy occurring—provided that contraception is even used. But look at families today, all the fatherless children and single moms that exist because two people, many of whom claimed to 'love' one another, decided to have sex without any commitment to form a permanent, stable family through marriage."

The student's face contorted with anger. "Marriage is permanent? Are you kidding me? What a joke." He stood up. "My mom has been divorced *twice* already. Most of my friends' parents are divorced. Believe me, marriage doesn't guarantee anything."

He looked away from the preacher. The plaza was emptying as the lunch crowd slowly dispersed. Nearby, oblivious to everything around them, a couple he recognized from the university campus leaned against the side of the fountain kissing.

The pain and disgust on the student's face was clear. The preacher's heart went out to him.

"That's true," the preacher said. "Marriage is only as good as people's commitment to keep it. I'm sorry to hear about your mom. That must have been very difficult for her—and for you."

"Yeah, well, it is what it is. I'm not interested in vowing to stay with someone for life when it's not likely to happen." Feeling embarrassed at the strength of his reaction, the student sat down again.

"And what would you do if your girlfriend got pregnant?"

"Not *marry* her."

"Okay, I realize this is a touchy subject—but my point is that the Bible says sex before marriage is wrong partly because it's not a loving choice for two people to demand the pleasure of sex if they aren't prepared to form a loving and stable place for any children that might be born out of that relationship. And we haven't even talked about the emotional wounds or STDs and so on…" The preacher paused and then spoke more softly. "If you really *did* love your girlfriend, wouldn't you want what's best for her, and not want to put her—and a possible future child—at risk of living in tragic circumstances?"

The question shook him. As if he didn't feel bad enough about his relationship, the preacher seemed determined to pour salt into the wound. He felt betrayed and violated by this man whom he had come to trust and regard as a friend.

"I thought we were having a conversation here," he interjected angrily. "I don't need to be lectured on my personal life! I've made decisions and I'm prepared to live with the consequences. They aren't yours or anyone else's to make!"

The preacher nodded. "Truthfully, I'm not trying to make your choices for you. I'm simply appealing to common sense with respect to your question about sex before marriage."

"Well, we don't need to discuss my personal life to do that."

"We don't have to."

The young man stood up. "I think we've gone as far as we need to go with this discussion anyway."

He regretted the words almost before they were out of his mouth, but he was too angry and humiliated to take them back. He turned his back on the preacher and struck out across the nearly deserted plaza in the direction of home.

The preacher watched the young man walk away in silence. He had a momentary urge to call out and plead with him, but he wanted to respect his feelings. The preacher knew his words had elicited a great deal of pain in the young man's heart—pain that had probably been there for some time. He had made a calculated risk, believing that if the young man was going to discover the truth, he first needed to confront the truth about himself. He wondered if he had made the right decision.

A part of him wasn't prepared to see their relationship come to an end—if, indeed, this was the end. He had grown more attached to the young man than he wanted to admit. It had been a long time since a young man had been granted entry to his heart.

Fourteen years, to be exact.

CHAPTER TEN:
Echoes

The following weeks found the preacher alone on the bench. His lunchtime ritual was nothing new, of course. For years, the preacher had used this time to pray, to divulge his pain, his joys, and his longings.

But since his meetings with the student ended, he had found it increasingly difficult to pray. He also found himself growing increasingly moody and irritable—even with his wife, who normally brought out his tender side. She had made some suggestions about his apparent sadness, but he was quick to dismiss them.

He knew what lay behind it. He knew that despite his best efforts to quell the disappointment and pain, he was angry at God. He was angry because this most recent loss echoed and magnified the pain of another—one he knew would never completely heal. Not in this life. The question that rose in his heart with great furor, the one he wanted to scream at God, was simple: *Why did you let this happen to me again?*

In his early meetings with the student, he had been careful to keep his heart in check, taking refuge in the intellectual tone of their conversations. As time passed, he couldn't deny his attachment to the young man had grown stronger. The student's growing affection for him also seemed unmistakable. Secretly, the preacher had begun to wonder if God had brought the young man across his path for a purpose beyond their weekly conversations…

But now all seemed lost. For the first few weeks following their final meeting, he harboured a hope that the young man would return and things would continue as before. He saw clearly that he'd been wrong to use his knowledge of the young man's relationship with his girlfriend to make a point, and he longed to apologize for his insensitivity.

As the weeks turned into a month, and then two, and the sky greyed over with cloud, his hopes faded. In a few days he would be forced indoors and his lunchtime ritual would cease. He dreaded the prospect of a winter made doubly bitter by loss.

He rose slowly, pausing to allow the faint pain in his back to finish its familiar arc, then turned and began the short walk to the church. Buffeted by wind, a few stray pages of newspaper tumbled across the near-deserted plaza, reminding the preacher of the tumbleweeds he'd seen on a family trip to Arizona many years ago. The memory only magnified his sadness.

<hr />

The student sat at the kitchen table and reread the paragraph in his Psychology text. He was trying to study; mid-terms were only a few weeks away and he had been taking extra shifts at work, limiting his study time. From the adjoining room, he could hear the faint but pitiful sounds of his mother's quiet sobbing.

She was having one of her "times," and as always, although he knew there was nothing he could do to help, he was plagued by guilt. And anger. His mother had been off work for several weeks, unable—or unwilling—to leave the house, although she dutifully dressed for work each morning, donning the blue smock and apron she wore during her cleaning shifts at the nearby motel. He tried his best to make up for the financial shortfall but was growing increasingly exhausted and frustrated by the demands of work and school. The financial burden weighed heavily.

Not that he wasn't used to handling things. He had been handling things—including caring for his emotionally troubled mother—for as long as he could remember. His only respite had come in the form of his mom's first husband, a kind man who was patient with her fits of depression and hysteria; he had cared for the two of them until his mother drove him away.

What he remembered most about that time were the ball games. Every Saturday his stepdad had taken him to the nearby park where they sat together eating hot dogs and rooting on whichever team seemed to be the underdog. Afterward, they would stop for a soda on the way home and recount their favourite game moments with laughter. His mom and stepdad had only been married a couple of years, but he often reflected back on that time as the happiest of his life.

As he thought about the kind man who had shown such interest in him, his thoughts turned to the preacher and their conversations over the past summer. He was seized, once again, by a deep sense of regret at his behaviour. He had been angry and hurt; his sense of pride had kept him from seeking the preacher to apologize or renew their discussion. As the summer faded and he found himself busy with a new semester at school, he increasingly felt as if he had made a terrible mistake.

He sighed and pushed his textbook away. With so much on his mind, he clearly wasn't going to get any studying done. Glancing at the clock, he saw that he had to be at the pizzeria in an hour. Deciding to get an early start, he quickly donned his work clothes and jacket and went outside.

His neighbourhood was located adjacent to a large suspension bridge in a poorer section of downtown. The rusting grey outline of the bridge seemed to increase his sense of loneliness and despair. He pulled his hood over his head to ward off the cold.

Two years earlier, he had taken a summer job with a contractor who was renovating some of the older houses in the neighbourhood. He had no experience to speak of, having been taught the basics of painting by a middle-aged Australian man who was hired at the same time.

One afternoon, the man related that his last job in Australia had been to paint a bridge, much like the one that loomed over the steeped-roofed houses they were busy renovating. When he asked the man how long the job had taken, the painter replied that he'd worked on the bridge almost three years. When he expressed surprise that painting a bridge should take so long, the man went on to explain that the bridge only took a year to paint from end to end, but by the time it was finished it was in need of painting again, so his crew simply returned to the other side to start over.

He had been dumbfounded. How could someone spend their life painting the same bridge over and over again? It seemed like an exercise in futility. Although he didn't understand it at the time, the image had touched a deep fear in him. Now, whenever he looked at it, the bridge was a dark and foreboding sign. As he headed into the inviting busyness of the city centre, he was grateful to leave the shadow of it behind him, if only for a little while.

CHAPTER ELEVEN:
Sutures

The student sat with his hands in his lap. He had tried crossing his legs, folding his hands; no matter how he sat, he felt awkward and uncomfortable as he waited on the hard-backed wooden chair facing the receptionist. From time to time she looked up from her computer monitor and acknowledged him with a faint but warm smile. The room was silent except for the soft mechanical sound of fingers typing on a keyboard.

To his right, a small wood-framed window looked out on the street where people scurried about like frightened animals, clutching their coats tightly about them, eager to escape the cold. Then he saw another figure moving more slowly. It was the figure of a man, head bent and moving with a deliberate but uneven gait. Instead of continuing down the length of the street, the figure turned and walked directly toward the window, growing larger before passing out of sight beneath the ledge.

The student's heart began to beat frantically. He looked at the secretary, then at the door. He could rush out without saying a word, or tell the secretary he had to leave and come back another time. Before he could make up his mind, he heard the metallic clack of the doorknob and the creak of the heavy wooden door he had entered twenty minutes earlier.

"You have a visitor." The secretary smiled at the figure, now hidden behind the open door. The door swung closed.

The figure turned. A look of surprise, followed quickly by delight, contorted his kind but worn face.

"Oh!" For a moment, it was all the preacher could manage.

The student froze, a surge of panic sweeping over him at the uncertain greeting. Perhaps he had offended the preacher when he stormed off. Perhaps the preacher wished he hadn't come. Maybe the best thing would be for him to leave... He stood, placing his hand on the doorknob.

"I'm sorry, maybe I shouldn't have come. I know we... uh, I know things didn't go so well last time..."

"No, no no!" The preacher's face betrayed a mixture of sincerity and fear. "Please, please... it's good to see you. I'm glad you came." He held out his hand, smiling.

The student shook it. There was something conveyed in the preacher's eyes—in the way they fixated and rested upon him—though he couldn't guess what it might be.

"Why don't you come into my office?" the preacher offered, wanting to escape the receptionist's knowing smile. She was aware of their lunchtime meetings in the summer and had sensed the impact the young man had been having on the preacher. She had also noticed the sadness and the restlessness that had manifested when their meetings ended.

"Sure."

The preacher opened the door to his office and escorted the student into the rather plain but cosy room. The first thing that struck the young man was the absence of pictures on the wall. Though the office was nicely furnished, the walls were stark and bare. The only picture frame in the room rested on the preacher's desk, a small brass frame like the one his mom kept his high school graduation photo in.

As the preacher settled into the chair behind his desk, he knew the first order of business was to apologize to the young man. Before he could find the words to begin, the young man spoke.

"I noticed … I noticed you have a cane against the wall over there." The student inclined his head toward the cane. "I've never seen you use one before."

"No, not in quite a while," the preacher replied. "I keep it to remind myself of how far the Lord has brought me."

The student winced at the reference to God, surprised as at other times by the vague sense of discomfort that arose within him.

"Do you mind if I ask what happened?" The student waited for a response, but none came. "How you got your limp?"

This line of discussion blindsided the preacher. The mixture of emotions he felt at seeing the young man again now mingled with a new and equally powerful flow of feelings. He took a deep breath.

"I was in a car accident many years ago," the preacher began slowly, "and broke my back. The doctors told me I would never walk again." Images flashed through his mind in rapid succession, some eliciting more pain than the memory of his prognosis.

"Obviously they were wrong."

His tone grew sombre. "Yes, they were."

A moment of awkward silence passed between them.

"So how did it happen? I mean, how did you begin walking again?"

"Well, I struggled on my own for a time." The preacher paused, aware of how great an oversimplification that was. "And then—and then I called out to God." He exhaled heavily. "I prayed. My wife prayed. Our congregation prayed. Then, one morning, I found I could stand."

The preacher felt vaguely lightheaded. He reached across the desk and grasped a half-finished glass of water he had left earlier in the day. He brought it to his lips and took a drink.

The student was nervous, but transfixed. He sensed his question had elicited powerful memories. While part of him felt regret at having blundered by asking such a deeply personal question, another part felt honoured by the preacher's willingness to divulge what was clearly a painful chapter in his life.

The preacher placed the glass back down. "Over a period of weeks and months, I could walk with less and less difficulty."

The student recognized that the preacher would have regarded his recovery as an answer to prayer—a miracle.

"What did the doctors say?"

"They couldn't explain it. They said I was very lucky."

"I bet you don't think luck had anything to do with it," the student suggested.

A satisfied smile stole across the preacher's face. "No, I don't. I believe God answered my prayers—and the prayers of many others. That's why I keep the cane. To remember that with God, anything is possible."

The student acknowledged the preacher's words with a nod. He had heard someone once say that a person with an experience was never at the mercy of a person with an argument. He knew that was true. The preacher would probably never be talked out of believing his recovery was a miracle. He had prayed and God had answered. It might not be true, but it was difficult to refute—especially when the evidence sat right there before him.

"Are we returning to our discussion about miracles?" the preacher replied, half-jokingly.

The student smiled. "I don't think so, no." His thoughts turned back to the preacher's accident. He tried to imagine the details surrounding it. Had there been another car involved? Had it been raining? He didn't want to pry, but his curiosity had been aroused. "Were you by yourself when it happened—the accident, I mean?"

The preacher's smile dimmed perceptibly. "No, there were two others in the car with me. My wife and…"

The preacher glanced over at the single picture frame on his desk. He reached out and took it carefully in his hand, the picture still not visible to the young man.

"My son."

"Were they injured?" The question was logical. Obvious. But instantly the student felt a stab of regret for asking it; the moment he uttered it, he saw the preacher wince.

"My wife was unhurt—just scratches and bruises." Still holding the frame, the preacher looked out the window in his office. From where he sat, he could see the tiny figures of pedestrians hurrying up and down the street. Without looking back, he added, "My son was killed."

The student sat in stunned silence. The preacher's words seemed to hang in the air—words with such weight it seemed they would solidify and come crashing down on their heads.

"I'm so sorry. I didn't realize…"

The preacher looked down and shook his head. "No, it's okay. It's okay." His face was bright red, as with the force of holding back a torrent of emotions. After a few moments, the pain seemed to drain from his expression. His eyes pierced the student with sudden directness and strength. "Not everything in life turns out the way we would like, but that doesn't mean it's the end—even if it feels like it at the time."

The preacher's words seemed so confident, so final— as if there were no other truth in the universe. The student was shocked.

How could someone have faith in God after losing a son? he wondered.

A deep, seething anger began to rise in him—as if all the injustices he'd ever seen or experienced suddenly floated to the surface.

"But how can you say that?" he blurted out. "How can you look at something so horrible and just accept it?" He felt angry and sad and confused and embarrassed all at the same time. "If there's a God, why would He let stuff like that happen? How could you serve a God who let your son die... and then healed *you*? It doesn't make any sense! How could you still be a Christian? Doesn't God care? Why didn't He *do* something!? Why *doesn't* He do something?"

The student shook his head and looked away. Tears streamed down his face, but he didn't care. He didn't know what it was like to lose a son, but he had lost things. Plenty of things. A stepfather he loved. A father he had never known. His mother's time and affection. He knew that many of his friends' stories were the same—or worse. The magnitude of it all infuriated him. It was as if the world was drowning in sorrow and God stood idly by, watching it all happen, unwilling to do anything, unwilling to lift a finger to help.

God certainly hasn't performed any miracles for me, he thought bitterly.

The preacher sighed. He could feel the tears forming in his own eyes—tears for the student, tears for himself. Tears for a son who had never lived to experience the joy of graduating from college, or marrying, or becoming a father. Tears for his wife, who had lost the child she had carried in her own body. Tears for the homeless people who endlessly streamed to the church for food and clothing until the day they stopped coming and it dawned on him that they would never come back.

It was a lot for anyone to deal with—all this loss. He looked over at the young man, whose grief and anger was laid bare before him, who was only now beginning to come to grips with the magnitude of his own losses. The preacher could only guess at them—but he sensed they were many, even at his young age. And he knew more would follow.

Life is, in one sense, a long litany of losses. He had said that in a sermon once. "Naked I came from my mother's womb and naked I will depart." That was how Job had described it. No matter how much we possess in this life, we eventually lose it all. And yet he also knew that life was far more than loss. There was also hope.

It was hope that had sustained him after the loss of his son, when he was confined to a bed for months on end, wrestling with his grief, wrestling with his faith, wrestling with his own shattered body. He walked to the window and looked out, as if to draw strength from without. If only he could convey some of this hope to the young man.

God, give me the words, he prayed silently.

He turned to the young man.

"My friend—" He had addressed the young man that way before, but now it seemed appropriate and deeply true. "There

119

is more to life than suffering and loss. I survived that horrible mess because I believe God *did* do something, and because He *will* do something. Because I have hope."

Hope. For the young man, the word held about as much substance as a deflated balloon. It was a term religious people used as if to imply that all one needed in life was something to hold onto. Like a life raft or a pain pill. My son died... but I have hope. My stepfather left... but I have hope! Hope in what? Hope for what? For a dead son to come back to life? For a stepfather to come home? Hope hardly seemed adequate compensation for a dead son or a fatherless existence.

"Listen, I don't mean any disrespect," the student replied, wiping his tear-streaked face, "but I don't see any *reason* for hope. Things happen, and God—if He exists—lets them happen! That doesn't exactly inspire me to believe things are going to get better. And it doesn't change reality, does it? We have to live in this stinking, messed-up world. If God is up there somewhere and He's so *good*, why isn't He doing something about all the crap that's going on *down here*?"

The preacher nodded. He knew exactly what the young man was talking about. He had struggled with the same question. Given the pain the student had experienced, the answer might be very difficult for him to accept.

"You know, in our discussions this past summer, we talked about what we could expect if God exists." He paused, waiting to see if the student would interject. He didn't. "I think what you said is true: we could expect God to do something about our screwed-up world."

The student was taken aback. The preacher seemed to have painted himself into a corner. He hadn't objected during his earlier rant when he had stated God let bad things happen. And God obviously hadn't saved his son. In the student's mind, the expectation for God to act seemed to provide clear evidence that God did *not* exist—or at least, that if he did exist, he wasn't good. Either way, the fact that the preacher could make such a statement, and still be a person of faith, was irritatingly contradictory.

"So if God exists, he should be doing something," the student replied. "No argument there. But the *point* is, it doesn't look like he's doing anything."

"I would have to agree with you," the preacher replied matter-of-factly. "That's exactly how it looks sometimes. But that doesn't mean he isn't doing anything, or doesn't have plans to fix things. And that, my friend, is the great hope of the Bible and the Christian faith—that God is going to fix things, and has, in fact, already begun."

"Really? How is that?"

The preacher sat forward and folded his hands. "The Bible promises that one day God will judge mankind. At that time, he will remove all sin and evil from the world, along with all pain and suffering and death. He will then set up an eternal kingdom on the earth where the righteous will live forever."

The student realized he'd heard this before, though he couldn't remember when or from whom. "You're talking about heaven."

"Not exactly. Heaven is where believers go when they die— *until* that day comes. Then heaven will come to earth."

"I always thought Christians believed they'll live in heaven forever."

"Well, that's more or less true—it's just not the whole story. But that's the source of our hope: a better life. A life without pain and suffering. Life as it was meant to be."

The student tried to imagine such a world. He realized he could not. But could he deny that he longed for such a place? Who didn't? It was either true, or it was a pipe dream. But there was no denying its power upon the imagination. He wondered if there was such a place, and if he belonged there…

"Okay, but that's all in the future. What I want to know is what's God doing in the meantime. Are we supposed to bank everything on heaven and tough it out until then?"

"Not at all," the preacher replied. "Do you remember when we talked about how the world is screwed up, and how our cups are nearly empty?"

"Sure."

"Well, part of what God is doing right now is filling our cups."

The student looked at him sceptically. "What do you mean?"

"Jesus said, 'Let all who are thirsty come to me and drink.' He was inviting people to come and be filled—to receive what they're looking for. To reunite them with the Source of life."

The student reflected on their previous conversation. "You mean love."

"Yes, love and everything else—peace, joy, the ability to love others. Everything humanity is lacking."

"So people receive those things by coming to Jesus?"

"Yes. Because Jesus' mission was to reconnect people to their purpose: which is to be in right relationship with God. When a person's relationship with God is restored, they begin to experience fulfillment and joy. They get a taste of what's to come. They start to experience heaven *right now*."

The student sighed. It was a lot to take in. Despite how crazy it seemed, it was impossible to deny that the preacher's cup was fuller than his own.

"Do you believe your son is in heaven?" he asked suddenly.

The question was blunt, but honest. His insensitivity was easy to excuse.

"Yes, I do."

"Because he was a Christian?"

"That's right."

"So, not everyone goes there…"

"No, I don't think it makes sense to believe that."

"Why not? I mean, why not a better world for everyone?"

"Because not everyone will choose to accept God's conditions."

"Which are?"

"The willingness to turn from sin and follow Christ."

The student looked doubtful. "But why would following Christ be part of the requirement? Can't people choose to do what's right without becoming a Christian?"

The preacher shook his head. "The Bible says Jesus was sent to earth to die for the sins of humanity. It also says very clearly that we cannot please God or earn eternal life through any effort of our own. It's God's gift. All that's required on our part is to receive it, to trust in what He's done, through Christ, on our behalf."

The preacher sighed. There was so much more he wanted to explain. He could feel fear rising in him, fear that their time together was somehow limited, that the young man would be lost to him and he wouldn't have another chance to say all he wanted to say…

The student wrestled with the preacher's words. They were difficult to accept, but he resisted the temptation to respond. It seemed the longer they talked, the more questions arose. The rollercoaster of emotions he'd experienced over the past thirty minutes were beginning to take their toll. He felt weary and weak and sad. He felt like he was on a journey and had travelled a thousand miles only to discover that he had just begun.

Seeing that their conversation was winding down, the preacher seized the opportunity. "Listen, ever since our last meeting I've wanted to apologize to you for hurting you the way I did. I should never have questioned you about your girlfriend like that."

The student looked mildly surprised at the admission.

"It was insensitive and wrong," the preacher added. "I hope you'll forgive me."

"Sure. It's no problem." The young man looked down. "And... I'm sorry that I stormed off the way I did."

"I understand. How *are* thing with your girlfriend, by the way?"

The student sat up in his chair. "I broke up with her."

"I'm sorry to hear that."

"No, it's fine. I didn't love her, so I thought it was only fair to let her know."

"How did she handle it?"

"Okay, I guess. Better than I expected."

"I see."

Aware their time together was coming to an end, there was something the preacher wanted to do, something he had been thinking about since he'd first seen the student waiting for him in the foyer.

He opened his desk drawer. Inside was a small black box. He opened it carefully.

Inside was a bronze medal with an inscription.

His son had won it at the all-county swim meet in his senior year of high school. He'd always been an exceptional swimmer and it had been his dream to win a medal in his favourite event—the 100-metre freestyle. Just a year before he died, he accomplished his dream, taking first place at what was to be his last meet. The preacher had never seen him so elated—and alive—as he had been that afternoon.

It had always been a beautiful thing to watch him swim. It was as if he had been born to do it. The preacher had kept the medal close to him all the intervening years, and it seemed that a part of his heart remained tied to his son through it. He also sensed that somehow, in a way he couldn't explain, his attachment had kept him from loving people the way he knew he could, from letting others in.

He held out the small black box. "I want you to have this. It was my son's."

The student stood.

With his free hand, the preacher turned the brass picture frame toward the student.

In it was a photo of a young man in a graduation robe and cap. He had dark hair, striking blue eyes, and a smile like the preacher's—sincere and kind.

The student was aghast. He backed up.

"No, I can't take it. It was your son's. I couldn't…"

The preacher smiled warmly, his hand still extended.

"No, you have it. I've held onto this for too long. It's yours now."

The student accepted the gift and the preacher walked over to the window and looked outside. A few snowflakes were falling, the first of the season.

"Think of it as my way of saying thanks for our talks together."

The student examined the medal in his hand. He suddenly wished he had something to give in return, something that would express how much their talks had meant to him. If he was honest, he would have to admit it wasn't the content of their conversations that he appreciated most. It was the closeness. Somehow being in the preacher's presence made him feel stronger, older. He realized that it was during their conversations he had felt like a man for the first time in his life.

He opened his mouth to speak, but his bottom lip began to quiver dangerously. He bit it. The preacher seemed to sense what was unspoken between them and placed a hand on the young man's shoulder. The young man laughed abruptly and looked down, embarrassed and amused at his discomfort.

The student tucked the small black box into his pocket. "Thanks so much for this. I really appreciate it."

"My pleasure," the preacher replied, squeezing his shoulder with affection.

"You know…. you know I haven't bought the whole Christianity thing yet."

The preacher smiled. "I realize that."

"And I still have a lot of questions."

"I'm sure you do. I'd love to help you out with them—if I can."

The student nodded. The preacher's gaze was loving and direct. And there was something else there—a brightness and depth of feeling he hadn't seen before, as if a window had suddenly opened up in the preacher's soul.

"So, are you going to study for your Sunday sermon now?" the student asked, feeling awkward, not knowing how to conclude their time together.

The preacher glanced out the window. "No, I think I'm going for a walk. I've got some things to sort out—and pray about."

The student surveyed the preacher, this man who had lost a son, and wondered what kind of father he had been. He could only think his son had been one very lucky—no, blessed was the word. One very *blessed* young man.

PART TWO:
Signposts

A PERSONAL JOURNEY

S ometimes a journey of the head inexplicably evolves into a journey of the heart. This was true for the characters in our story, and it was certainly true for me. Although it undoubtedly began much sooner, in my university years I became increasingly aware that the answers our culture supplied for the questions I was asking were woefully inadequate. It was then that I first began to seriously consider the possibility that the answers I was looking for were wrapped up in the notion of God.

My journey began in earnest when I befriended a young woman who invited me to a Christian church. As my relationship with the young woman grew, so did my contact with these unusual "believers." Although a professed agnostic/atheist (I actually wasn't sure which best described my ever-changing stance on the subject of God), I was impressed and intrigued by the sincerity and depth of faith I observed in this group of deeply committed Christians.

Even more compelling was the deep love that characterized their relationships. In fact, it contrasted so profoundly with everything I'd ever experienced that I was initially dismissive, unable to believe that such decent, wholesome, and loving people were actually to be found in the world.

In time, it became clear that I was wrong. Although I couldn't doubt their sincerity, I continued to doubt the truth of what they believed. After all, I knew it was possible to be sincere but wrong, and I had no interest in adopting a system of belief simply because it "worked," because it gave me a false sense of comfort or security or love. I wanted to know the truth, and I had great misgivings about the Bible and the claims of Christianity.

Around that time, a certain woman in the church challenged me to put my misgivings to the test—to examine and research the Bible for myself—and loaned me a book to get started. The book was filled with scholarly research about the Bible and the historical person of Jesus Christ. I hesitated. Partly out of laziness (did I really want to do a bunch of additional research when the demands of school were already so pressing?) and partly out of fear (what if I discovered it was true and had to change my life?).

There was also a third, equally troubling consideration threatening to stop me before I even began. Like the student in our story, I was keenly aware that Christianity was only one possibility among many and I was daunted by the prospect of investigating the entire spectrum of world religions. All of a sudden, one book turned into countless more, perhaps a life-time of searching, all without any guarantee of success.

Was there any way to narrow the possibilities? If God had spoken to man, where was I most likely to find Him? What signs might distinguish the "true" religion from all the others? As I pondered these questions, I let reason and common sense guide me. As I did so, I began to see that some basic assumptions could be made which helped narrow the possibilities and perhaps point me toward the truth.

These assumptions were hardly airtight, but I began to suspect that the truth shouldn't be too difficult to discover. Given the opportunity already before me to investigate one of the world's great monotheistic religions, I wanted to begin with the confidence that I was starting in a logical place.

As I reflected on these assumptions, it became clear that some religions were better candidates than others, and Christianity was certainly among them. So I continued to attend church. I also began to research the Bible and examine the teachings and claims of Christianity, as well as those of other religions. At the same time, I couldn't help but be affected by what I saw and experienced among the believers I'd become acquainted with. And so I began to open my heart—as well as my head—to whatever signposts God may have chosen to leave in this world to point me to the truth.

I invite you to do the same.

As you well recognize by now, the assumptions and questions which guided me formed the basis for the conversations between the preacher and the student. I offer this second section as a means to reconnect with them and apply them in your own search for truth.

Let me state clearly that I'm not an expert in world religions. Although some basic facts about various religions are mentioned in this book, it is not intended as a study of world religions. I leave that task to you, if you so desire. Rather, the premise of this book is that the truth of God should be accessible to ordinary people. I believe this because the world is full of ordinary people, and God, if He exists, knows this. It makes sense to believe that God would make the truth about Himself relatively easy to identify—at least to those who are genuinely looking. By genuinely looking, I mean individuals who are willing to adjust their lives to the truth when they find it. As the preacher in our story suggested, it's easy to feign interest in the truth until we are confronted with the need to respond to it.

As a professed Christian for the past nineteen years, I make no claim to complete objectivity. As with the preacher in our story, my own beliefs are an open book. However, it may help you to know that it was through a process similar to the one outlined in this story that I came to be a Christian (not the other way around). I'm a Christian because I'm deeply convinced that Christianity presents the truth about God. That's the head side. There's also a heart side, which I have alluded to. But I leave you to formulate and follow your own conclusions.

If you're an agnostic, this book was written with you in mind. If you're an atheist, I encourage you to seriously consider the assumptions and questions discussed in this book in light of a statement made by Stephen J. Gould, one of the foremost proponents of evolutionary theory before he passed away in 2010: "Science simply cannot... adjudicate the issue of God's possible superintendence of nature."[1] From a purely scientific or intellectual point of view, the issue of God's existence, as

Gould suggests, is perhaps unresolvable. And yet we can—and will—formulate beliefs about God, the universe, and ourselves. We must. Because life demands it. Because this is the time we have in which to choose. Only let us choose carefully.

If you're a religious person, I encourage you to consider the evidence presented in this book and apply the questions reiterated in this last section to your current religious faith and consider the implications carefully.

If you're a Christian, I believe you'll be encouraged to discover that from a common sense perspective, Christianity has much to commend it.

Most of all, I encourage you to be a truth-seeker. The Bible suggests that those who seek truth with all their heart will find it. I believe there's no better prerequisite to discovering truth than a sincere desire to know and follow it, no matter the cost or implications. I believe truth is everything, that without it we are truly lost, and that discovering and following it is the first great responsibility of man.

IT ALL BEGINS WITH PURPOSE

Once we begin to consider the possibility of God's existence, the first logical question is this: where is the truth about God to be found? In a world replete with conflicting perspectives on God and God's relationship with man, the question can seem daunting. However, as the preacher suggested early in our story, some basic assumptions might be made which can help answer this question.

Strictly speaking, each of these assumptions would be prefaced by a statement along the lines of, "If there is a God who is omnipotent, omnipresent, and good, it is reasonable to assume that…"

Assumption #1: God created humanity for a purpose. If God exists, the universe is His handiwork—and so are we. Which means that we are here for a *reason*. Whatever motivated God to bring us into being, within that motivation lies our purpose, our reason for being.

Assumption #2: God would be willing and able to communicate that purpose to us. If God created humanity, it doesn't make sense to believe that He would intentionally leave us in the dark about the single most important piece of information we could possibly possess or desire. As the preacher suggested, it would be like making us a lock while withholding the key. The idea that God might withhold our purpose because "it's the search for truth that really matters" is equally illogical. That would be like saying it's the search for food that really matters, and not *eating*! For God to create humanity and then deliberately withhold our purpose from us would be inexplicably cruel, and not at all consistent with the nature of a benevolent God.

Some people also postulate that it's impossible to know God because we're incapable of perceiving or interacting with Him. Perhaps God would like to communicate with us, but we simply cannot perceive or understand Him. This is faulty logic. If God is all-powerful, it would certainly be within His power to communicate with us on a level we could understand. To suggest His power is limited in this way would be to strip Him of His deity.

Assumption #3: God would be able to preserve the record of His divine revelation (message) to man over time. Another common argument is, "Perhaps God has spoken to humanity at some point in time, but His message has been twisted and corrupted by people." This argument again suggests some limitation on God's part. Any being worthy of the name of God would surely be capable of preserving any message He delivered to humanity over the course of time, despite human attempts to corrupt it. It only makes sense that if God has indeed spoken to man, that message has been preserved *intact*. After all, why would God go to the trouble of delivering truth to us and then allow that truth to be distorted or nullified when He would clearly be capable of intervening to prevent it? It just doesn't make sense.

Assumption #4: A large portion of humanity would eventually be drawn to a true revelation from God. Since a true revelation from God would contain the answers to our deepest and most significant questions, it is reasonable to assume that in time, a large portion of mankind would come to recognize the significance of this revelation. Consequently, we wouldn't expect a true revelation from God to be doomed to obscurity, with only a handful of people "in the know." Rather, we would expect it to eventually be embraced by many people. And with thousands of years of human history behind us, it is almost incomprehensible to suppose that God hasn't *already* spoken. Therefore, it makes sense to believe that such a revelation has already been given and has likely found expression in one of the world's great religions. Considering them would therefore be a logical starting point for anyone searching for the truth about God.

TOO MANY GODS

One of the most common statements heard in our culture concerning world religions is that they're are all "basically the same." Depending on the perspective of the individual making the statement, the connotation is either positive (they all teach similarly helpful morals and values) or negative (they're all out to lunch).

However, while we seem content to pay collective lip service to this perspective, two things seem abundantly apparent. First of all, the people who know these religions best (their followers) clearly disagree. To say that religion has been a source of conflict in the world is an understatement. And secondly, as the preacher in our story pointed out, anyone who's intellectually honest would be forced to admit that despite any apparent similarities, the religions of the world are very contradictory, both in their depiction of God and His requirements for humanity.

The reality is that the various views of the world's religions are hopelessly irreconcilable. One religion commands its followers to persecute and oppress those who oppose its message and refuse to convert; another commands them to forgive and bless their enemies. One religion prescribes human sacrifice to please the gods; another condemns such practices as evil and demands that mercy and kindness be shown to all people. One is monotheistic; another is polytheistic. Still another is atheistic. Trying to smooth it all away by claiming that they're all "basically the same" only confuses the matter further for those who are genuinely interested in discovering the truth.

Another common argument is that God is painting a picture of Himself through all world religions—like a face that emerges from the seemingly disparate pieces of a mosaic. It suggests that each religion has a "part" of the truth; this was the personal view of Gandhi. It's an appealing idea, to be sure, but not at all practical. After all, how are we supposed to determine which part of each religion is right or wrong? It makes far more sense to believe that God would simply give us the truth in a clear and straightforward way.

No, all religions are not the same, nor can they all be true. But since it makes sense to believe that God would make the truth known to us, it is likely that *one* of them represents the truth. It also makes sense to believe God would provide us with a way of distinguishing the true religion from the others—with "signposts," if you will, to point us in the right direction.

UNLIKELY CANDIDATES

As mentioned in our story, given our foundational assumptions, it's clear that certain religions represent unlikely candidates for a revelation from God based on their own foundational claims. Atheistic religions, for example, can be ruled out since it would be illogical to suggest God would deliver a revelation denying His own existence. Religions that take an agnostic stance (such as Buddhism) are also suspect since they provide no definitive revelation of God at all. Pantheistic religions are problematic, both in terms of their logical consistency and in that they posit a viewpoint at odds with our basic definition of God as the omnipotent, omnipresent, and omniscient being responsible for creating the universe.

Furthermore, religions that permit or encourage self-contradictory or illogical views, such as those which accept other (naturally incompatible) religion systems as equally "true," or permit contradictory stances among their followers (such as the freedom to be a monotheist, polytheist, or pantheist—as is the case within Hinduism) would represent unlikely candidates, as would those which make no claim to constitute divine revelation. For such reasons, several world religions are ruled out as likely candidates within the context of our story. However, recognizing that some would object to dismissing a major world religion on the basis of a single line of reasoning, I encourage you to examine any religion you deem worthy of consideration in light of the ideas presented in this book.

What follows is a brief review of the assumptions and "signposts" discussed in our story, along with some corresponding questions for reflection.

SIGNPOST #1:
Personal Transformation.

Assumption: A true revelation from God will produce profound, positive transformational change in the lives of those who embrace it.

Since a revelation from God concerning man's purpose would contain the answers to our deepest questions and longings, it makes sense to believe that it would produce deep transformational change in the lives of those who embrace it. Practically speaking, we would not expect the "true" religion to be a religion of ritual adherence only, but a religion of *effect*. We would expect it to elevate, inspire, and heal human beings in a unique and unprecedented way and to stand out clearly from the others.

Questions for reflection. If you're a religious person, have you experienced profound personal transformation as a result of practicing your current religion? Or has its impact been only nominal?

Have you encountered any individuals who were eager to share their account of how religion transformed their life? If so, to what religion did they subscribe?

Which world religion displays the strongest evidence of profound, positive transformational change in the lives of its followers?

SIGNPOST #2:
Positive Global Impact

Assumption: A true revelation from God will transform the world for good.

True personal transformation inevitably brings about transformation on a larger scale. As more and more individuals are enlightened, their light begins to make a difference in the world at large. Simply stated, we would expect a revelation from God to be beneficial, increasing rather than decreasing the amount of good in the world. (It is important to note here, that by their very nature, most religions will display *some* evidence of having made a positive impact on both individuals and society at large. In fact, much good has come into the world from places outside of religion altogether.) We would expect the "true" religion to stand out significantly from the others, having impacted the world in an unprecedented way.

Question for Reflection. Which religion of the world has most impacted the world for good?

SIGNPOST #3:
The Supernatural

Assumption: A true revelation from God will be accompanied by supernatural evidence.

Most religions believe in the concept of divine (supernatural) intervention. Both as an indicator of divine action and as a way of distinguishing a true revelation from God from false ones, we would expect evidence of the supernatural to correlate closely with the true religion. Conversely, we would expect false revelations (or religions) to lack the confirming fingerprint of significant supernatural evidence.

Questions for Reflection. Which religion displays the most credible ongoing evidence of the supernatural?

Among the religions which claim evidence of miracles, which of them display miracles that highlight God's benevolent nature and thereby point people to God? Which of them display miracles that seem more like parlour tricks, than displays of God's nature and power?

SIGNPOST #4:
A Credible Messenger

Assumption: A true messenger of God will possess moral credibility.

Many religions have a primary prophet or founder who claimed to have received a revelation from God. We would expect individuals chosen to be messengers of God to live lives consistent with God's own nature. In short, we would expect them to have moral credibility. As the preacher said, if someone claimed to be a messenger from God but lacked those qualities—or demonstrated qualities that otherwise contradicted God's nature—we would have good reason to question their claim, as well as their message.

Questions for reflection. Which prophets/founders claim to be recipients of a revelation from God?

Which prophet/founder of a world religion possesses the highest degree of moral credibility, evident both in their teaching and personal conduct?

SIGNPOST #5:
Inclusivity

Assumption: A true revelation from God would be inclusive.

Since all human beings share a common purpose, we would expect a true revelation from God to apply and be relevant to all people. We would expect it to transcend gender, ethnicity, and socioeconomic status—even education and intelligence. For it not to would be unjust. After all, why would a benevolent God doom a person to a purposeless existence or exclude them from the divine plan on the basis of factors over which they have no control? We would therefore expect the true religion to preach a message for 'everyman' and demonstrate success in its ability to draw followers from all backgrounds, ethnicities, and walks of life.

Questions for reflection. Which religions of the world have a message that's truly inclusive?

Which world religion best demonstrates inclusivity in terms of its ability to draw followers from all background, ethnicities, and walks of life?

SIGNPOST #6:
A Credible Worldview

Assumption: A true revelation from God will provide the best explanation for life as we know it.

A worldview is simply a concept of the universe and how it works. Consciously or not, we all subscribe to some type of worldview. Whether religious or secular in nature, every worldview provides specific answers to the questions we choose to ask about the universe, ourselves, and God.

We would expect a true revelation from God (and its corresponding worldview) to reveal our purpose and provide a sufficient explanation for the many facets of human existence and experience. We would expect it to shed light on the reasons for good and evil, sorrow and joy, tragedy and triumph, and ecstasy and suffering. Not only would we expect it to provide an explanation for these things, we would expect it to provide the *best* explanation, since it represents the truth and not merely a theory or someone's "best guess."

Question for reflection. Which religion espouses a worldview most in keeping with the observed reality of human life and existence?

SIGNPOST #7:
Salvation

Assumption: A true revelation from God would reveal God's desire and/or intentions to resolve the problems of humanity.

Perhaps the most commonly asked question in relation to God is, "If there's a God, why is there so much suffering in the world?" The question implies two reasonable assumptions about the nature of God: 1) that God (if He is good) would care about the ills of humanity, and 2) that He would be willing (and able) to do something about them. It makes sense to believe God would not intend to simply leave the world as it is, but that He would act to fix it. It's also reasonable to expect that He would communicate and/or demonstrate this intention to us in any revelation He should choose to deliver.

Questions for reflection. Which religion(s) reveals/demonstrates God's desire and willingness to bring healing to the ills of humanity?

Which religion's concept of salvation appears to most deeply answer the needs and longings of humanity?

SIGNPOST #8:
Agreement with Conscience

Assumption: A true revelation from God will promote a lifestyle consistent with conscience.

Although not explicitly discussed by the characters in our story, it's clear that the true religion ought to project a morality in agreement with universally recognized precepts of conscience (a prohibition against murder, theft, adultery, etc.). Any religion which espoused or encouraged practices to the contrary or provoked serious issues of conscience within its followers would naturally be suspect.

Questions for reflection. Which religion promotes a lifestyle most consistent with universality accepted precepts of conscience?

Which religions appear to promote practices which are morally questionable (violence, discrimination, injustice, etc.)?

DOES ONE RELIGION STAND OUT FROM THE OTHERS?

In my own search for the truth, it became apparent that the first religion I encountered up close—Christianity—had some very impressive credentials to commend it as the truth. But don't take my word for it. I invite you to consider the following facts and quotations concerning Christianity in light of the assumptions and signposts we've just reviewed.

BY THE NUMBERS

The following chart illustrates the estimated numbers of followers of various religions worldwide.[2] As the preacher indicated, you will notice that the numbers drop off dramatically after Buddhism, and that the four top religions—Christianity, Islam, Hinduism, and Buddhism—dwarf the remainder of the world's religions in terms of numbers of adherents. While estimates vary, a quick online search of these figures demonstrate that there's little or no doubt regarding Christianity's ranking among world religions. It's easily the world's leading religion, with roughly a third of the world's population describing themselves as followers.

While this alone certainly doesn't prove Christianity represents the truth about God, it does indicate that the Christian faith has been embraced—and is regarded as truth—by more people than any other religion in the world.

Religion	Members
Christianity	2 Billion
Islam	1.2 Billion
Hinduism	785 Million
Buddhism	360 Million
Judaism	17 Million
Sikhism	16 Million
Baha'i	5 Million
Confucianism	5 Million
Jainism	4 Million
Shintoism	3 Million
Wicca	.7 Million
Zoroastrianism	.2 Million

Note: Information gathered by the U.S. Central Intelligence Agency (CIA) indicates that as of 2009, 33.35% of the world's population were Christian; 22.43% were Muslim; 13.78% were Hindu; 7.13% were Buddhist, and 0.6% were Sikhs. (By comparison, only 2.04% of the world's population were atheists.)[3]

CHRISTIANITY & SIGNPOST #1:
Personal Transformation

The Bible says...

> This means that anyone who belongs to Christ has become a new person. The old life is gone; a new life has begun! (2 Corinthians 5:17, NLT)

> ...you were cleansed; you were made holy... (1 Corinthians 6:11, NLT)

> At one time we too were foolish, disobedient, deceived and enslaved by all kinds of passions and pleasures. We lived in malice and envy, being hated and hating one another. But when the kindness and love of God our Savior appeared, he saved us... (Titus 3:3–5, NIV)

The most immediate and compelling evidence Christianity has to offer in terms of its claim to represent the truth about God is without question the transformed lives of individuals who have responded to its message. If you live in the western world, you've likely heard testimonies from Christians either firsthand or on the airwaves. The alcoholic who is now sober because of Christ. The gang member who is now a pastor. The workaholic father who's reformed his ways and become devoted to his family. The list goes on. Simply google "Christian testimonies" and you'll find thousands of webpages staring back at you, filled with compelling real-life accounts of people whose lives have been dramatically altered by the Good News of Jesus Christ.

But are they for real? Paradoxically for some, the sheer volume and similarity of such accounts can have a numbing effect on the psyche and foster doubts about their authenticity. Allow me to offer a personal anecdote which may give you some idea of how legitimate and common such transformations truly are. I personally know many individuals whose lives were transformed after they responded to the Christian message. Let me tell you briefly about four of them.

The first was a street fighter, alcoholic, and distributor of black-market porn whose nickname was "Animal." The second was an alcoholic and drug addict who once threatened to burn down a Christian church. The third was a controlling and domineering husband whose behaviour contributed to his wife's growing problem with alcohol and prescription drugs. The fourth was a drinker and brawler who wandered from place to place and was frequently in trouble with the law. Each of these individuals, in the thick of their sinful lifestyles, encountered the message of Christ and responded. Some years later, I served with these four Christian *leaders* on the staff of my home church.

The alcoholic and drug addict became our Children's Pastor, and went on to lead his own congregation several years ago. The domineering husband (recently retired) became our church's Marriage Pastor and Counsellor. Together with his wife, he worked to build and heal marriages within the Christian and secular community for more than twenty years. The man who had trouble with the law became our Associate Pastor, planted a church in Moscow after the collapse of the Berlin Wall in 1992, and now pastors a church near Toronto, Canada. And the man once known as "Animal"? He became a fiery preacher, eventually founding the two-thousand-member church I called home for many years. Today this man is also a spiritual father to many Christian pastors and leaders and presides over a ministerial network of more than four hundred churches and ministries in Canada.

Despite their troubled pasts, each of these individuals are not only law-abiding citizens today, but respected both in their churches and in their communities as exemplary leaders. Each would tell you without a moment's hesitation that the changes that took place in their lives were the result of one thing and one thing alone: their encounter with Jesus Christ. Keep in mind that these examples of transformed lives are from the leadership of a single church among hundreds of churches in one city of two hundred thousand people. That's not to mention the scores of other individuals who have been transformed within this church, or in the millions of other churches worldwide.

I hope you're getting the picture. Those who dare to investigate the impact of Christianity where it counts—in the lives of individuals who take its message to heart—will discover that its impact is both real and impressive. Whereas it might be difficult to quantify such transformation, as you read the upcoming section on global impact, keep in mind that any impact Christianity has had is due to its ability to transform lives on an individual basis.

What others have said...

> In [the disciples] was a power, a life, which came to them through Jesus and which worked moral and spiritual transformation. That power, that life, proved contagious.
>
> —Kenneth Scott Latourette, American historian and author of the two-volume *A History of Christianity.*

One thing that has confirmed to me the resurrection of Jesus Christ two thousand years ago is the transformation of the lives of millions of people when they become related by faith to the person of Jesus. Although they are from every walk of life and from all the nations of the world, they are charged in remarkably similar ways. From the most brilliant professor to the most ignorant savage, when one puts his trust in Christ, his life begins to change.[4]

—Christian apologist Josh McDowell, who converted to Christianity after attempting to disprove it

It must be noted that the early Christians, who were persecuted for three centuries, never set out to change the world. The changes largely occurred as a by-product of their transformed lives…[5]

—Alvin J. Schmidt, professor of sociology, and author of *How Christianity Changed the Word*

CHRISTIANITY & SIGNPOST #2:
Global Impact

What the Bible says…

When Jesus spoke again to the people, he said, "I am the light of the world…" (John 8:12, NIV)

You are the salt of the earth… You are the light of the world… let your light shine before others, that they may see your good deeds and glorify your Father in heaven. (Matthew 5:13–14, 16, NIV)

And I... when I am lifted up from the earth [on the cross], will draw and attract all men... to Myself. (John 12:32, AMP)

The impact Christianity has had on the world—and on the western world in particular—is one of its most glowing credentials. Beyond all question, Christianity has fulfilled Jesus' own prediction of being a light to the world. It is the often unrecognized source of much of the humanitarianism seen both in the West and around the world.

What others have said...

It is impossible to exaggerate the importance of the coming of Christianity. It brought with it, for one thing, an altogether new sense of human life. Where the Greeks had demonstrated the powers of the mind; the Christians explored the soul... they taught that in the sight of God, all souls were equal, that every human life was sacrosanct and inviolate... Where the Greeks had identified the beautiful and the good, had thought ugliness to be bad, had shrunk from disease as an imperfection and from everything misshapen as horrible, and repulsive, the Christians... sought out the diseased, the crippled, the mutilated, to give them help. Love, for the ancient Greek, was never quite distinguished from Venus... for the Christians held that God was love, it took on deep overtones of sacrifice and compassion.[6]

—American historian R. R. Palmer (1909–2002)

On the basis of historical evidence, I am fully persuaded that had Jesus Christ never walked the dusty paths of ancient Palestine, suffered, died, and risen from the dead, and never assembled around him a small group of disciples who spread out into the pagan world, the West would not have attained its highest level of civilization, giving it the many human benefits it enjoys today. One only needs to look to sectors of the world where Christianity has had little or no presence to see the remarkable differences.[7]

—Alvin J. Schmidt

The greatest religious change in the history of mankind... [took place] under the eyes of a brilliant galaxy of philosophers and historians who disregarded as contemptible an Agency [Christianity] which all men must now admit to have been... the most powerful moral lever that has ever been applied to the affairs of men.

—British historian W.E.H. Lecky

This man's [Jesus'] unique and exemplary life, and his suffering, death, and physical resurrection from the dead transformed his handpicked disciples as well as the lives of many others... The lives that he transformed in turn changed and transformed much of the world: its morals, ethics, health care, education, economics, science, law, the fine arts, and government.[8]

—Alvin J. Schmidt

Christianity is the greatest civilizing, molding, uplifting power on this globe.

—American educator Mark Hopkins (1802–1887)

CHRISTIANITY & SIGNPOST #3:
The Supernatural

Concerning the resurrection of Jesus, the Bible says...

> I passed on to you what was most important and what had also been passed on to me. Christ died for our sins, just as the Scriptures said. He was buried, and he was raised from the dead on the third day... He was seen by Peter and then by the Twelve. After that, he was seen by more than 500 of his followers at one time... (1 Corinthians 15:3–6, NLT)

> That Sunday evening the disciples were meeting behind locked doors because they were afraid of the Jewish leaders. Suddenly, Jesus was standing there among them! "Peace be with you," he said. As he spoke, he showed them the wounds in his hands and his side. (John 20:19–20, NLT)

What others have said...

> The bodily resurrection of Jesus Christ from the dead is the crowning proof of Christianity... If the resurrection did not take place, then the Bible is false and

Christianity is a false religion. If it did take place, then Christ is God and the Christian faith is absolute truth.[9]

—Henry Morris (1918–2006), former professor of Applied Science and co-founder of Christian Heritage College and the Institute for Creation Research

I know of no one fact in the history of mankind which is proved by better, fuller evidence of every sort than the great sign that Christ died and rose again from the dead.

—British educator and historian
Thomas Arnold (1795– 1842)

It was therefore impossible that [the disciples] could have persisted in affirming the truth they have narrated, had not Jesus actually risen from the dead, and had they not known this fact as certainly as they knew any other fact… The resurrection of Christ is the most verifiable fact of ancient history.

—Simon Greenleaf, founder of Harvard School of Law

As a lawyer, I have made a prolonged study of the evidences for the events of the first Easter. To me, the evidence is absolutely conclusive. Over and over in the court I have secured the verdict on evidences not nearly so compelling.

—Sir Edward Clarke, nineteenth-
century lawyer and politician

It has been shown... that the disciples truly believed and taught that the risen Jesus had appeared to them. Further... numerous additional evidences also indicate that there actually were such appearances... The visual claims of the earliest eyewitnesses are therefore vindicated: the most likely explanation is that the same Jesus who had recently died had been raised from the dead and had actually appeared to his followers, both individually and in groups. The data shows that the disciples witnessed actual appearances of the risen Jesus, which they faithfully reported in a historically ascertainable fashion.[10]

—Gary R. Habermas, Distinguished Research Professor, Liberty Baptist Theological Seminary and Graduate School

Concerning Jesus' miracles, the Bible says...

A vast crowd brought to him people who were lame, blind, crippled, those who couldn't speak, and many others. They laid them before Jesus, and he healed them all... Those who hadn't been able to speak were talking, the crippled were made well, the lame were walking, and the blind could see again! (Matthew 15:30–31, NLT)

That evening many demon-possessed people were brought to Jesus. He cast out the evil spirits with a simple command, and he healed all the sick. (Matthew 8:16, NLT)

What others have said...

The tradition that Jesus was someone who performed marvels is too deeply rooted in the New Testament, and can be traced to such an early date, that most scholars conclude that the only explanation to account for this tradition is that marvels did occur. Eliminate all references to miracles in the gospel pages and there is no gospel left. It is a simple historical fact that both friend and foe saw Jesus as a wonderworker.[11]

—H.J. Richards

Virtually all ancient miracle stories outside the Bible are described in texts written long after the events they report. But we read the stories of Jesus' works in documents composed within a generation of his life, by people who claimed to see the events, and in a context where friends and foes alike could either confirm or dispute the stories. By contrast, the story about the Buddha flying and shooting sparks, for example, is from [a]… text dating many centuries after Buddha's life.[12]

—David K. Clarke

Despite the difficulty which miracles pose for the modern mind, on historical grounds it is virtually indisputable that Jesus was a healer and an exorcist.[13]

—Marcus Borg, theologian and prominent member of the Jesus Seminar

For these miracles the historical evidence is excellent.[14]

—A.M. Hunter, on Jesus' ability to heal the blind, deaf, and others

In light of the evidence for the historicity of Jesus' miracles in the Gospels, few scholars today would attempt to explain these events as purely the result of legend or myth.[15]

—Daniel Morais and Michael Gleghorn

But Jesus' works… are unlike magic in that he performed miracles by his own power and authority. In biblical miracles, God graciously responded to requests for supernatural help. By contrast, magic generally involves manipulation of spiritual, perhaps demonic forces.[16]

—David K Clark

Concerning miracles within contemporary Christianity, the Bible says…

These are some of the signs that will accompany believers: They will throw out demons in my name… they will drink poison and not be hurt, they will lay hands on the sick and make them well. (Mark 16:17–18, The Message)

When the crowds heard Philip [a disciple] and saw the signs he performed, they all paid close attention to what he said. For with shrieks, impure spirits came out of many, and many who were paralyzed or lame were healed. (Acts 8:6–7, NIV)

Most people are unaware that claims of profound miracles abound not only within the lives of Jesus' first disciples (as described in the book of Acts) but within the context of present-day churches and Christian Gospel Crusades around the world. What follows are a sampling of claims of miraculous healings along the lines of what Jesus himself performed from a single Gospel ministry based in South Africa. Keep in mind that these claims are from one such ministry among many thousands which exist to carry the Christian message to people in diverse parts of the world.

On Monday, 12 September [2011], Dieudonne Kayumba of the DRC's [Democratic Republic of Congo] Makungu village heard the Gospel and received Christ. Later, Dieudonne testified that he was also healed that night of hip, back and knee problems that had plagued him for a year. By Friday of that week, he was rejoicing because he was not only still healed, but was also experiencing freedom from sins he had turned from...[17]

...Augustin Ngoyi, a fifteen-year-old boy in the Mpande village of the DRC... had been suffering with an external hernia for three years. He had only known to turn to local witchdoctors, none of whom could help him, and the condition only got worse. After receiving Christ at the outreach, Augustin also received prayer healing. He later testified that the external hernia had disappeared and he is finally free of pain.[18]

Geoffrey Omariba had been unable to sit upright due to a back disorder. Last month at a Gospel

Outreach in Kenya's Sibanga village, Geoffrey testified of being totally healed.[19]

Rose Wanyama rejoiced as she testified that a tumour disappeared from her stomach while she prayed the prayer of salvation. This tumour had been in her stomach for the past 10 years.[20]

—Burton Karuri, Kenya

Patrick Wafula who is 62 years old suffered from vab-normally high fevers and from severe pain in the joints of his legs. When he came to a meeting he was experiencing a very high fever and was in great pain. As Patrick prayed for salvation God touched him and his temperature normalised and all the joint pain disappeared.[21]

—Burton Karuri, Kenya

CHRISTIANITY & SIGNPOST #4:
A Credible Messenger—Jesus Christ

The Bible says...

Why then do you accuse me of blasphemy because I said, "I am God's Son"? Do not believe me unless I do what my Father does. But if I do it, even though you do not believe me, believe the miracles, that you may know and understand that the Father is in me, and I in the Father. (John 10:36–38, NIV)

Which of you can truthfully accuse me of sin? And since I am telling you the truth, why don't you believe me? (John 8:46, NLT)

And you know that God anointed Jesus of Nazareth with the Holy Spirit and with power. Then Jesus went around doing good and healing all who were oppressed by the devil, for God was with him. (Acts 10:38, NLT)

What others have said…

The fact is that we have better historical documentation for Jesus than for the founder of any other ancient religion.[22]

—Edwin Yamanuchi

I know men and I tell you that Jesus Christ is no mere man. Between Him and every other person in the world there is no possible term of comparison. Alexander, Caesar, Charlemagne, and I have founded empires. But on what did we rest the creation of our genius? Upon force. Jesus Christ founded His empire upon love; and at this hour millions of men would die for Him.

—Napoleon

Two thousand years ago there was One here on this earth who lived the grandest life that ever has been lived yet—a life that every thinking man, with deeper or shallower meaning, has agreed to call divine.

—Frederick W. Robertson, nineteenth-century clergyman, on Jesus Christ

Jesus of Nazareth, without money and arms, conquered more millions than Alexander the Great, Caesar, Mohammed, and Napoleon; without science and learning, he shed more light on things human and divine than all philosophers and scholars combined; without the eloquence of school, he spoke such words of life as were never spoken before or since, and produced effects which lie beyond the reach of orator or poet; without writing a single line, he set more pens in motion, and furnished themes for more sermons, orations, discussions, learned volumes, works of art, and songs of praise than the whole army of great men of ancient and modern times.

—Historian and theologian Philip Schaff

Whatever may be the surprises of the future, Jesus will never be surpassed.

—Ernest Renan, French historian,
religious scholar and linguist

I am a historian, I am not a believer, but I must confess as a historian that this penniless preacher from Nazareth is irrevocably the very center of history. Jesus Christ is easily the most dominant figure in all history.

—H.G. Wells, British writer and historian (1866–1946)

[Jesus'] life is the most influential ever lived on this planet and its effect continues to mount.[23]

—Kenneth Scott Latourette, former President of American Historic Society, in *A History of Christianity*

How, in the name of logic, common sense, and experience, could an imposter—that is a deceitful, selfish,
depraved man [Jesus]—have invented, and consist-
ently maintained from the beginning to end, the purest
and noblest character known in history with the most
perfect air of truth and reality? How could He have
conceived and successfully carried out a plan of unpar-
alleled beneficence, moral magnitude, and sublimity,
and sacrificed His own life for it, in the face of the
strongest prejudices of His people and age?

—Philip Schaff, on the possibility that Jesus
deliberately deceived people as to his identity

It was reserved for Christianity to present to the world
an ideal character which through all the changes of 18
centuries has inspired the hearts of men with an impas-
sioned love; has shown itself capable of acting on all
ages, nations, temperaments and conditions; has been
not only the highest pattern of virtue, but the strongest
incentive to its practice.... The simple record of these
3 short years of active life has done more to regenerate
and soften mankind than all the disquisitions of philosophers and all the exhortations of moralists.

—William Lecky, British historian and dedi-
cated opponent of organized Christianity

Unlike the leaders of... other religious movements,
Jesus was no political figure... Yet he changed millions more than Alexander the Great, Mohammed,
and Napoleon put together. It all happened because

his message and his physical resurrection transformed his early followers, who did not pick up the sword to defend themselves even during brutal persecutions, but rather they were about spreading his love and the need for his forgiveness by word and deed to all—regardless of race, sex, ethnicity, poverty, or wealth.[24]

—Alvin J. Schmidt

CHRISTIANITY & SIGNPOST #5:
Inclusivity

The Bible says...

Therefore, go and make disciples of all the nations, baptizing them in the name of the Father and the Son and the Holy Spirit. (Matthew 28:19, NLT)

In Christ's family there can be no division into Jew and non-Jew, slave and free, male and female. Among us you are all equal. That is, we are all in a common relationship with Jesus Christ. (Galatians 3:28, The Message)

After this, I saw a large crowd [in heaven] with more people than could be counted. They were from every race, tribe, nation, and language, and they stood before the throne and before the Lamb [Jesus]. They wore white robes and held palm branches in their hands... (Revelation 7:9, CEV)

The global reach of Christianity can be easily seen through a simple ranking of the largest Christian populations world-wide.[25] Notice that the top ten spots include nations from North America, South America, Europe, Asia, and Africa—every populated continent except Australia, whose total population is too small to qualify it for a high ranking.

Countries	Estimated 2010 Christian Population	Percentage of Population That is Christian	Percentage of World Christian Population
United States	246,780,000	79.50%	11.30%
Brazil	175,770,000	90.2	8.0
Mexico	107,780,000	95.0	4.9
Russia	105,220,000	73.6	4.8
Philippines	86,790,000	93.1	4.0
Nigeria	80,510,000	50.8	3.7
China	67,070,000	5.0	3.1
DR Congo	63,150,000	95.7	2.9
Germany	58,240,000	70.8	2.7
Ethiopia	52,580,000	63.4	2.4
Subtotal for the 10 Countries	1,043,880,000	40.4	47.8
Total for Rest of World	1,140,180,000	6.3	52.2
WORLD TOTAL	2,184,060,000	31.7	100.0

What others have said...

Christianity is today more widely distributed geo-graphically and more deeply rooted among more people than it or any other faith has ever been.[26]

— Kenneth Scott Latourette, American historian and author of the two-volume *History of Christianity*

CHRISTIANITY & SIGNPOST #6:
A Credible Worldview

The Bible says...

In the beginning God created the heavens and the earth. (Genesis 1:1, NIV)

And we know that the Son of God has come, and he has given us understanding so that we can know the true God. (1 John 5:20, NLT)

The God who made the world and everything in it is the Lord of heaven and earth and does not live in temples built by hands... From one man he made every nation of men, that they should inhabit the whole earth; and he determined the times set for them and the exact places where they should live. God did this so that men would seek him and perhaps reach out for him and find him, though he is not far from each one of us... Therefore since we are God's offspring, we should not think that the divine being is like gold or silver or stone—an image made by man's design and skill. In the past God overlooked such ignorance, but now he commands all people everywhere to repent. For he has set a day when he will judge the world with justice by the man he has appointed. He has given proof of this to all men by raising him from the dead. (Acts 17:24, 26–27, 29– 31, NIV)

I first examined the Bible and the claims of Christianity as a university undergrad studying English and minoring in philosophy. Having been exposed to the teaching of many of history's greatest philosophers, I'd come away disheartened. No single system of thought seemed capable of providing a satisfying explanation for the richness and diversity of human life and experience. However, as I studied Jesus' teaching, I was stunned by His insight into human nature and the human condition. In the Bible, I found for the first time a plausible explanation for the bewildering and seemingly contradictory array of experiences, feelings, and longings that characterized my own life and human experience on the whole.

No teaching, perspective, or philosophy I had ever encountered so closely correlated with this life *as we actually experience it*. In the Bible, I found the explanation for joy and sadness; for triumph and tragedy; for hope and despair; for love and guilt; and most all, for the source of the discontent and longing that had prompted my search in the first place. Here I found, in one system of thought, a logical, compelling, and comprehensive explanation for the total sum of human reality and experience.

Given my disparaging view of religion at the time, the thought that such profound and glaringly true answers could be found within the pages of a religious text rather than a philosophical treatise had never occurred to me, but I couldn't deny it; Christianity had provided me with the best explanation I had ever encountered for the life I lived and the world I was living in.

What others have said…

> Christianity is not a series of truths in the plural, but rather truth spelled with a capital "T." Truth about total reality, not just about religious things. Biblical Christianity is Truth concerning total reality—and the intellectual holding of that total Truth and then living in the light of that Truth.
>
> — Francis Schaeffer, American theologian and philosopher (1912–1984), in his Address at the University of Notre Dame, April 1981

> The Christian worldview gives the most satisfying answer to the question, *How do you explain human nature?* The Bible teaches that God created us to be His image-bearers, which makes us distinct from the entire rest of creation. But when Adam and Eve chose to rebel in disobedience, their fall into sin distorted and marred the sacred Image. The fact that we are created in God's image explains the noble, creative, positive things we can do; the fact that we are sinners who love to disobey and rebel against God's rightful place as King of our lives explains our wicked, destructive, negative behavior. It makes sense that this biblical view of human nature reveals the reasons why mankind is capable of producing both Mother Teresa and the holocaust.[27]
>
> —Sue Bohlin

I am totally convinced the Christian faith is the most coherent worldview around... When you think of it... really there are four fundamental questions of life. You've asked them, I've asked them, every thinking person asks them. They boil down to this... How did I come into being? What brings life meaning? How do I know right from wrong? Where am I headed after I die?

When you take the answers of Christ to those four questions, there is no parallel that brings individually, correspondingly, true answers to those individual questions. And then you put the four together, there's no other world view that brings such a coherent set of answers... The person of Christ is so unique that no honest seeker can deny it once you have looked at his answers to these questions.

In the Hindu worldview, it is sort of karma, inherited, every birth is a rebirth, you pay, you pay, and you pay through millions of incarnations. In the Muslim worldview, it's fatalistic—it's the will of Allah. You go on. There's no real down-to-earth explanation. It's just there. Within the Christian worldview, there is a plethora of evidence as to how Jesus defends for us the reality of evil and the reality of good. When you go to the cross, you see the two converge—evil in the heart of man, goodness in the heart of God. That convergence in the cross of Jesus Christ is so unique that it even prompted Mahatma Gandhi to say outside of the cross, he did not know where else something so unique could be given as an answer.[28]

—Ravi Zacharias, Indian-born Christian apologist and visiting professor at Oxford University

CHRISTIANITY & SIGNPOST #7:
Salvation

What the Bible says…

The Spirit of the LORD is upon me, for he has anointed me to bring Good News to the poor. He has sent me to proclaim that captives will be released, that the blind will see, that the oppressed will be set free, and that the time of the LORD's favor has come. (Luke 4:18–19, NLT)

And we have seen and testify that the Father has sent his Son to be the Savior of the world. (1 John 4:14, NIV)

For God loved the world so much that he gave his one and only Son, so that everyone who believes in him will not perish but have eternal life. God sent his Son into the world not to judge the world, but to save the world through him. (John 3:16–17, NLT)

Then I saw a new heaven and a new earth, for the old heaven and the old earth had disappeared. And the sea was also gone. And I saw the holy city, the new Jerusalem, coming down from God out of heaven like a bride beautifully dressed for her husband.

I heard a loud shout from the throne, saying, "Look, God's home is now among his people! He will live with them, and they will be his people. God himself will be with them. He will wipe every tear from their eyes, and there will be no more death or sorrow or crying or pain. All these things are gone forever."

> And the one sitting on the throne said, "Look, I am making everything new!" And then he said to me, "Write this down, for what I tell you is trustworthy and true." (Revelation 21:1–5, NLT)

Among the Bible's unifying themes, perhaps the greatest of these is God's desire to restore humankind to its original place and purpose in His design. In the first book of the Bible, we glimpse the first two humans, Adam and Eve, living in harmony with their Creator and with each other in Paradise. We witness their act of disobedience to God, their banishment from Eden and the Tree of Life, and the consequences that quickly follow: they experience fear for the first time, find themselves hiding from God, and within a generation the first murder occurs—Cain kills his brother Abel, and soon after the world is engulfed in violence. This is the world with which we are intimately familiar—a world gone wrong.

Within the remaining books of the Old Testament, divinely appointed messengers begin to speak of a coming kingdom, in which God himself will rule the earth with justice. And after many years, Jesus appears, announcing that God's kingdom has come at last! True to His proclamation, He speaks words that transform sinners into saints and performs miracles that set men's bodies and souls aright. But suddenly, after a mere three years of public ministry, He is murdered and all seems lost.

But wait! His disciples began to proclaim that He is alive! Death, it seems, couldn't hold Him. Jesus then appears to His disciples and reveals that the miracles He performed are just a foretaste of what is yet to come, that the kingdom won't fully come until people the world over have been invited to accept

God's invitation to eternal life, until the Gospel (the Good News) of the kingdom has been preached to the whole world. Then He ascends to heaven.

Finally, in the last book of the Bible, penned by the last surviving of Jesus' original Twelve disciples, we get a glimpse of what God has had in mind all along: mankind is back in Paradise. Both man and the earth have been restored to their original state of perfection. There is no more suffering or pain. No more sin, death, or injustice. Man has access to the Tree of Life once again and lives forever. Does that sound like a fairy tale?

Perhaps, but as John Eldgredge remarked in *Epic*,

> What if all the great stories that have ever moved you, brought you to joy or tears—what if they were telling you something about the true Story into which you were born?[29]

The Christian conceptions of salvation and heaven are so compelling precisely because they answer the deepest longings of humanity in the most satisfying way imaginable.

What others have said...

> [Christianity] provides a unified answer for the whole of life.[30]
>
> —Francis Schaeffer

> What makes the miracle stories "gospel" [Good News] is not their historical accuracy, but their meaning. Their meaning first of all for Jesus, who interpreted the cures

that took place in response to his preaching as evidence that the kingdom of God was breaking in on the world... He saw the healing of the sick who crowded round him as part of his mission to make God's world whole.[31]

—H.J. Richards

[Jesus'] whole life was evidence of his own wholeness and freedom. He showed matchless insight into the deeper and hidden source of humanity's sickness, and had utter confidence in the will of God to rescue humans from the disintegrating forces that cripple their lives. Moreover, he was able to inspire others with the same confidence.[32]

—H.J. Richards

CHRISTIANITY & SIGNPOST #8:
Agreement with Conscience

Does Christianity promote a lifestyle in agreement with universally recognized precepts of conscience? Consider the following the sampling of Jesus' teachings and the teachings of the Bible.

Jesus taught His followers:

- To turn from evil. (Mark 1:15; Matthew 4:17)

- To love one another. (John 13:34–35; John 15:12,17)

- To love your neighbour as you love yourself. (Matthew 22:39; Mark 12:31)

- To do to others what you would have them do to you (the Golden Rule). (Matthew 7:12)

- To love your enemies and do good to them. (Matthew 5:44; Luke 6:27,35)

- Not to judge others. (Matthew 7:1; Luke 6:37)

- To give to the poor. (Matthew 6:3; 19:21)

- To clothe the naked, care for the sick, and feed the hungry. (Matthew 25:44–45)

- To give to everyone who asks. (Luke 6:30)

- To show mercy. (Matthew 5:7; 9:13; 18:33)

- To be at peace with your neighbour. (Mark 9:50)

- Not to lust. (Matthew 5:28)

- To be faithful in marriage. (Matthew 19:9,18)

- To forgive those who sin against you. (Matthew 18:21–22; Luke 11:4)

- Not to swear. (Matthew 5:34–37)

- Not to seek revenge, but turn the other cheek. (Matthew 5:39; 6:29)

- To not be hypocritical, but practice what you preach. (Matthew 23:3,27)

- To seek to serve others, rather than be served. (Matthew 20:26; Mark 10:45)

- To do good. (Matthew 5:16; 6:1)
- Not to be greedy. (Luke 11:39; 12:15)

Other teachings of the Bible:

- Don't steal. (Exodus 20:15)

- Don't lie. (Exodus 20:16; Leviticus 19:11)
- Don't envy. (Exodus 20:17; Deuteronomy 5:21)
- Don't murder. (Exodus 20:13; Deuteronomy 5:17)
- Children should honour their parents. (Exodus 20:12; Ephesians 6:2)
- Obey governmental authorities. (Romans 13:1; 1 Peter 2:13–14)
- Pay your taxes. (Romans 13:6–7)
- Honour others more than yourself. (Luke 14:10; Romans 12:10)
- Honour your elders. (1 Peter 5:5)
- Sympathize with the sorrows of others. (Romans 12:15; 1 Peter 3:8)
- Care for widows and orphans. (James 1:27; 1 Timothy 5:16)
- Don't be jealous or selfish. (Romans 13:13; Galatians 5:26)
- Don't slander others or gossip. (Romans 1:29; 1 Timothy 3:11)
- Don't get drunk. (Romans 13:13; Ephesians 5:18)
- Help others. (Galatians 6:10; 1 Thessalonians 5:14)

It's worth noting that all the precepts identified in Dr. Kent M. Keith's famous Universal Moral Code—fundamental moral principles found in societies around the world—are clearly expressed in the teachings of Jesus and the Christian Bible.[33]

What the Bible says…

> So they went out and preached that men should repent [that they should change their minds for the better and heartily amend their ways, with abhorrence of their past sins]. (Mark 6:12, AMP)

> Always let others see you behaving properly, even though they may still accuse you of doing wrong. Then on the day of judgment, they will honor God by telling the good things they saw you do. (1 Peter 2:12, CEV)

> But the Holy Spirit produces this kind of fruit in our lives: love, joy, peace, patience, kindness, goodness, faithfulness, gentleness, and self-control. There is no law against these things! (Galatians 5:22–23, NLT)

> And as for you, brothers, never tire of doing what is right. (2 Thessalonians 3:13, NIV)

THE CHRISTIAN MESSAGE:
An Appeal to Conscience

As Signpost 8 implies, truth and conscience are closely linked. I believe we know truth—including the truth about God and the state of our relationship with Him—when we encounter it because it appeals to us at a deep, instinctive level. Given our inherent need to perceive truth and discover our purpose, it makes sense to believe that God would give us the necessary tools to perceive truth even in the absence of extensive education and knowledge. I believe that one of these tools is our conscience.

Conscience is defined as "the inner sense of what is right or wrong in one's conduct or motives, impelling one toward right action."[34] In fact, the word is derived from two words: *con* (meaning "with") and *science* (meaning "knowledge"). Taken together, conscience indicates our human faculty of being inherently "with knowledge" of certain truths.

Those familiar with the opening words of the U.S. Declaration of Independence will recall that the framers began by stating their belief in certain self-evident truths. Every system of belief needs such a starting place, a belief in certain truths which, while perhaps not strictly provable, form a starting point. For Descartes, it was the *Cogito*. For the framers of the Declaration it was the equality of all people and the inalienable rights of life, liberty, and the pursuit of happiness.

While grounded in historical fact, the Christian message has always taken the form of an appeal to *conscience*, based on similar self-evident truths. These truths could be summarized as follows:

- All people are sinners (have done wrong).
- We *should* do what is right and good (and have failed).
- Wrong actions deserve punishment.

THE GOOD NEWS

Based on these self-evident truths, the message of Christianity could be explained very simply:

1. God is merciful and is willing to forgive people.

2. In return, God expects people to:

   i. Stop deliberately sinning and purpose to do what is right.

   ii. Have faith (trust, reliance) in God's forgiveness through Jesus Christ.

In short, the Christian message begins by pointing out what we can hardly hope to deny: that we screw up (a lot), that we *should* do what is right, and that wrong actions should have consequences. It then announces that what we desperately need is, indeed, available (God's forgiveness) and then outlines the conditions for receiving it.

WHY JESUS MATTERS

At this point, you may be wondering why the second condition—faith in God through Jesus Christ—is part of the requirement. One way to understand it is as follows. In terms of Jesus' place in the Christian message, the Bible says that Jesus played the role of facilitator in God's plan for humanity by providing the missing piece to the equation of God's forgiveness. You see, the principle that wrong actions deserve consequences isn't necessarily nullified by an offer of forgiveness—or a decision on our part to turn our backs on sin and reform our lives.

In the case of more serious crimes like rape and murder, it is easy to sympathize with the victim's family members when they demand that the perpetrator pay a price for their wrong actions, *even if they're remorseful*. It's harder when our own sins don't seem so serious in our own eyes, but the same principle still stands. Someone *should* pay. Justice, which has its origin in God's own nature, must be satisfied.

And the Bible tells us that someone did. It tells us that God Himself stepped up to the plate and paid the price *for* us, paving the way for His forgiveness to come to each of us. God became a man and took the punishment for our sins upon Himself. He was punished *in our place*. The Bible says that man was Jesus Christ. Although he *never* sinned, He was beaten, whipped, and then subjected to the most humiliating and painful form of death known in the ancient world—crucifixion. All for us. Then, so that His disciples and all who came after them would know for certain that He was no ordinary man, no mere prophet or teacher, and that the debt for sin was truly paid, God raised Him to life after three days.

But there's more. Before He was killed, Jesus lived a perfect life. He always did what is right, and in doing so he provided mankind (through both His life and teaching) with an example to follow. As a result, we no longer have to wonder how God's wants us to live or how to do what's right. Jesus showed us how.

For two very important reasons—that Jesus paid the price for our sins, securing God's forgiveness, and that God commands us to emulate (follow) Him in this life—the Christian message is expressed as "repent and believe in Jesus." Jesus is the way to live and the Bible clearly explains that to receive God's forgiveness, we must repent (turn from sin) and believe (trust in, follow) Jesus.

THE PROBLEM WITH "GOOD·DEEDS" RELIGIONS

Religions or belief systems that propose a "good deeds" way to heaven are as numerous as they are illogical. Why illogical? They're illogical because they don't require the necessary prerequisites for forgiveness—a reformed attitude toward our past wrong behaviours and a decision to live righteously. Think about it. The good deeds approach suggests that if my good deeds outweigh my bad deeds, I'll go to heaven. What that means, practically speaking, is that I'm still actually free to willfully choose to do evil anytime I want—as long as I make up for it by doing enough good deeds to balance the scales in my favour.

But that's like a convict testifying before the parole board that upon release he will continue selling drugs, but promises to balance his illegal activity by praying or volunteering at the local soup kitchen. How would we expect the parole board to respond to his request for an early release? Not favourably.

CHRISTIANITY IN SUMMARY

As the world's leading religion, Christianity is embraced as the truth by more than two billion followers worldwide. With large Christian populations on every continent, it's easily the most geographically and ethnically diverse religion in the world. There is significant evidence to suggest that the degree of moral beneficence it has imparted to both individuals and societies around the globe is unmatched by any religion past or present and its founder and divine revelatory, Jesus Christ, is regarded by both believers and non-Christians alike to be one of the world's most morally credible individuals and teachers. If judged by His impact on the world through the faith He founded, it's hard to dispute that Jesus is the most dominant figure in history.

Add to this the compelling historical evidence that Jesus did, in fact, work miracles that displayed God's benevolent intentions toward humanity with great feeling and clarity; evidence that He imparted this ability to some of His followers, who continue to perform wonders in his name today; and the historical basis for belief in His bodily resurrection from the dead, and you may begin to understand the worship and reverence His name evokes among Christians the world over.

Furthermore, Jesus' teachings, and the teachings of the Bible, not only encourage a lifestyle in keeping with universal precepts of conscience, but far exceed them. The essential message of Christianity—that people need to reform their wrong behaviour and seek God's forgiveness—cannot be disputed on grounds of conscience, nor can the underlying implication that *humanity* is the source of the world's woes, and that the world will not change unless human beings do.

Beyond all this, Christianity offers the world a justification for longing and hope—that God has, indeed, seen the world's woes, cares deeply about humanity, and has put into action a plan, centred on Jesus Christ, to fix both them and us, as well as to satisfy our deepest longings in the most spectacular way imaginable.

TAKE A CLOSER LOOK

Given its impressive resumé, I'm sure you will agree that anyone sincerely interested in discovering the truth about God cannot afford to ignore Christianity. As you have read, many of history's keenest minds have regarded both Christianity and its founder, Jesus Christ, as preeminent among world religions and their founders, past or present. At the very least, the Christian faith is worth investigating and represents a logical starting point for anyone sincerely interested in discovering the truth about God.

So how does one go about investigating Christianity? What follows are some practical ways to investigate the Christian faith firsthand.

Step #1: Pray. Since it makes sense to believe God wants us to know the truth about who we are, who God is, and why we are here, it only makes sense to enlist His help with discovering the truth! Of all the prayers we could pray, we can be certain He would wish to answer this one.

Step #2: Visit a church. Experience Christianity for yourself in the lives of those who are followers of Christ. And while you're there, watch their interaction with one another to get an idea of what a Christian community looks like in action. Talk to the Christians you meet and ask them questions you might have about what they believe and why they believe it. Listen to the message that's preached with an open heart and mind.

Be sensitive to the atmosphere and ask yourself, *Is God truly with these people?* Jesus predicted that His followers would be distinguished by joy and love for one another—hallmarks of God's presence among people. You may even wish to visit more than one church to judge the similarities and differences between various Christian communities.

Step #3: Investigate Christ's claims and teachings. The surest way for you to know what Christianity is truly about is to investigate the claims, teachings, and life of Jesus Christ firsthand by reading the Gospels (Matthew, Mark, Luke, and John). The first four books in the New Testament comprise different accounts and perspectives on Jesus' life and teaching. You might be surprised to discover that they're like four mini-novels, fascinating both in terms of their story and content. Pay close attention to Jesus' claims about Himself and ask yourself if they are supported by His life and teaching.

If a Bible is gathering dust somewhere in your house, chances are it's a King James Version—a seventeenth-century English translation that's almost unreadable today (unless you're a lover of Shakespeare). If you want to truly get a sense of what the Bible says, look for newer translations in modern English. The New International Version (NIV) and the New Living Translation (NLT) are excellent, as is the Common English Version (CEV). Very inexpensive Bibles can be purchased just about anywhere.

Step #4: Research. Investigate Christianity and/or other religions as desired. Many excellent resources are available online and in book form to help answer questions about Christianity, such as:

- Is the Bible true?
- How was the Bible written?
- Did the Bible change over time?
- Was Jesus a real historical figure?
- Are the Bible and science at odds with each other?

Feel free to consult the section entitled "For Further Study" for a short list of recommended books and online resources to help you get started in your investigation. You may also wish to investigate other religions (including ones we judged as unlikely candidates, such as Hinduism and Buddhism) and compare them with Christianity. Compare their worldviews and messages and apply the signpost tests identified in this book.

BORING CHURCH, HYPOCRITICAL PEOPLE

I realize that some who read this book may have had an experience with the Christian faith that left a bad taste in your mouth. Perhaps you've attended church services that were repetitive, boring, and lifeless. It's true that some churches and denominations within the Christian faith have become bound with tradition and ritual and no longer accurately portray the life and freedom Christ intended His followers to experience and demonstrate.

If this is true in your case, I strongly recommend you look elsewhere. Seek out a church in your area that stresses adherence to the teachings of Scripture and cultural relevance. Many churches have perceived the need to break with certain traditions and adapt an approach more closely aligned with the teaching of Christ and the lives of believers depicted in Scripture.

Perhaps you've encountered Christians who were clearly hypocritical in their lifestyle and behaviour. If you've been turned off by evidence of hypocrisy, I would encourage you to re-examine Christianity on the merits of Christ's teachings rather than the failings of His followers. While unpleasant to experience, hypocrisy is reflective of the human condition and an inevitable fact of life within every religion and system of belief.

Finally, be forewarned: it has become a kind of fashion within our culture (at least in North America) for people to call themselves "Christians" as a way of indicating any manner of belief in God or higher morality—ironically, even among followers of other religions! True Christians will be those who profess a relationship with God through Jesus Christ on the basis of having turned from their sins and expressed faith in Christ through obedience to His teaching and example.

READY TO FOLLOW?

At this point, most of you are liable to fall into one of three categories of individuals. There will be those who, as a result of considering the subject matter of this book, perceive the need to investigate Christianity and/or other religions further. I heartily encourage you to do so. There will be those of you who lack the interest or desire to pursue the subject of God any further (or have strong convictions which you are not prepared to change). Still others, on the basis of a deep conviction of your conscience, will recognize a need to respond to the Christian message. It is to this third group that I now speak.

The Bible proclaims that we are all sinners. It testifies that God's will is for us to do what's right, and that we have failed. It also points out that one day God will judge humanity for its sin, and that the consequence for our failure is punishment (in a "prison" called hell).

However, it also contains a marvellous promise, expressed in the most widely known verse from the Bible:

> For God so loved the world that he gave his one and only Son, that whoever believes in him shall not perish but have eternal life. (John 3:16, NIV)

Jesus paid the price for your sins on the cross and offers you God's forgiveness today—right now, in this moment. What He requires in return is that you repent of (turn from) your current lifestyle of sin and disobedience to God and put your trust in Jesus Christ. Believe in Him. Follow Him. Trust in what He's done for you.

When you do so, you'll not only receive God's forgiveness, but the promise of eternal life—an eternity in paradise with God and other believers! Furthermore, the moment you repent and believe in Jesus, the Bible says you'll be adopted as God's child, and He will come and live within you, giving you desires that mirror His own, and the *ability* to live a life that pleases Him.

Truthfully, that's just the start. God has promised so much more, but those are the basics. You can choose to repent of your sins and trust Christ at any moment—even right now. All you need to do is make a decision, then call out to Him and tell Him. If you're having trouble finding words, you can pray something like this,

> Dear God,
> Today I repent of my sins and choose to believe in and follow Jesus Christ.
> Please forgive me and help me to please you all the days of my life.

I give you my life, my obedience, and my future.
In Jesus name I pray,

Amen.

ADVICE FOR FOLLOWERS

Now that you've become a follower of Christ, God's will for you is that you *become more and more like Jesus* as you live out the remainder of your life here on earth. But you're going to need some help! You'll want to begin to do a number of thing as soon as you're able.

Find a church. Find a church that teaches from the Bible and encourages a personal relationship with God through faith in Jesus Christ. Here you will develop relationships with other Christians who can help you in your journey of faith and receive teaching that will help you become more like Jesus.

Be baptized. Jesus commanded that those who choose to follow Him be baptized in water as a sign of their commitment to repent of their sins and trust in Him. Some churches baptize every few weeks or months. Be baptized as soon as you're able.

Pray. The moment you choose to follow Christ, God becomes your Father. You have the privilege of talking to Him about anything and everything. Use it and pray!

Read the Bible. Start in the New Testament with the Gospels (Matthew, Mark, Luke, and John). In the Gospels, you'll learn about Jesus' life, teaching, and miracles. Read carefully and ask God to help you obey.

In all these things, pray for God's direction and help. You'll be surprised at how He answers your prayers and shows Himself to you.

SHARING THE JOURNEY

I invite you to share your thoughts and questions about this book and your own spiritual journey at www.concerninggod.ca.

If you've made the decision to become a follower of Christ as a result of reading this book, I'd love to hear about it, pray for you, and assist you in any way I can. You may contact me at www.concerninggod.ca.

FOR FURTHER STUDY

Recommended Books

Guillermo Gonzalez and Jay W. Richards. *The Privileged Planet* (Washington, DC: Regnery Publishing, 2004).

C.S. Lewis. *Mere Christianity* (New York, NY: Touchstone, 1996).

Josh and Sean McDowell. *More than a Carpenter* (Carol Stream, IL: Tyndale House, 2009).

Josh McDowell. *Evidence that Demands a Verdict* (Nashville, TN: Thomas Nelson, 1999).

Alvin J. Schmidt. *How Christianity Changed the World* (Grand Rapids, MI: Zondervan, 2006).

Lee Strobel. *The Case for Christ* (Grand Rapids, MI: Zondervan, 1999).

Daniel Taylor. *The Myth of Certainty* (Downers Grove, IL: InterVarsity Press, 1999).

N.T. Wright. *Simply Christian* (San Francisco, CA: Harperone, 2006).

Ravi Zacharias. *Jesus Among Other Gods* (Nashville, TN: Thomas Nelson, 2000).

Recommended Websites

Josh.org (http://www.josh.org/)

Ravi Zacharias International Ministries (http://www.rzim.org/media/)

Answersingenesis.org (http://www.answersingenesis.org/)

Alexmcfarland.com (http://www.alexmcfarland.com/)

The Poached Egg (http://www.thepoachedegg.net/)

Christian Apologetics & Research Ministry (http://carm.org/islam)

Islam Review (http://www.islamreview.com/)

ENDNOTES

1   Stephen J. Gould, "Impeaching a Self-Appointed Judge," *Scientific American*, July 1992, 267(1):118–121.

2   GodWeb. "The Top Dozen Religions of the World." Date of Access: June 7, 2012 (http://www.godweb.org/religionsofworld.htm).

3   Central Intelligence Agency. "The World Factbook: People & Society." Date of Access: June 7, 2012 (https://www.cia.gov/library/publications/the-world-factbook/geos/xx.html).

4   Josh McDowell and Bill Wilson. *The Best of Josh McDowell: A Ready Defense* (San Bernadino, CA: Here's Life's Publishers, 1990), p. 427.

5   Alvin J. Schmidt. *How Christianity Changed the World* (Grand Rapids, MI: Zondervan, 2006), p. 39.

6   R.R. Palmer and Joel Colton. *A History of the Modern World* (New York, NY: McGraw-Hill, 1995), pp.15–16.

7   Alvin J. Schmidt. *How Christianity Changed the World* (Grand Rapids, MI: Zondervan, 2006), p. 14.

8   Ibid., p. 16.

9   Institute for Creation Research. "The Resurrection of Christ—The Best-Proved Fact in History." Date of Access: January 17, 2013 (http://www.icr.org/ChristResurrection/).

10 Gary R. Habermas. "The Resurrection Appearances of Jesus." *In Defence of Miracles*. Ed. Douglas Geivett & Gary

R. Habermas. (Downers Grove, IL: Intervarsity Press, 1997), p. 275.

11 H.J. Richards. *The Miracles of Jesus: What Really Happened?* (Mystic, CT: Twenty-Third Publishers, 1986), p. 99.

12 David K. Clark. "Miracles in World Religions." *In Defence of Miracles.* Ed. Douglas Geivett & Gary R. Habermas. (Downers Grove, IL: Intervarsity Press, 1997), p. 211.

13 Marcus J. Borg. *Jesus, A New Vision: Spirit, Culture, and the Life of Discipleship* (San Francisco, CA: Harper San Francisco, 1991), p. 61

14 A.M. Hunter. *Jesus: Lord and Saviour* (Grand Rapids, MI: Eerdmans, 1976), p. 63.

15 Probe Ministries. "Did Jesus Really Perform Miracles?" Date of Access: June 13, 2012 (http://www.probe.org/site/c.fdKEIMNsEoG/b.4227257/k.3E6C/Did_Jesus_Really_Perform_Miracles.htm#text3).

16 David K. Clark. "Miracles in World Religions." *In Defence of Miracles.* Ed. Douglas Geivett & Gary R. Habermas. (Downers Grove, IL: Intervarsity Press, 1997), p. 210.

17 Jesus Alive! Gospel Outreach. "Gospel Outreach Impact." Date of Access: June 5, 2012 (http://www.jesusalivego.org/index.php?option=com_content&task=view&id=83&Itemid=78).

18 Ibid.

19 Ibid.

20 Jesus Alive! Gospel Outreach. "Furfural Village." Date of Access: June 5, 2012 (http://www.jesusalivego.org/

index.php?option=com_content&task=view&id=721&Ite mid=202).

21 Ibid.

22 Lee Strobel. *The Case for Christ* (Grand Rapids, MI: Zondervan, 1998) pp. 81, 86. Quoting Edwin Yamanuchi.

23 Kenneth Scott Latourette. *A History of Christianity, Volume One* (New York, NY: Harper and Row, 1975), p. 34.

24 Alvin J. Schmidt. *How Christianity Changed the World* (Grand Rapids, MI: Zondervan, 2006), p. 45.

25 The Pew Forum on Religion & Public Life. "Global Christianity: A Report on the Size and Distribution of the World's Christian Population." Date of Access: June 13, 2012 (http://www.pewforum.org/Christian/Global Christianity.exec.aspx).

26 Kenneth Scott Latourette. *A History of Christianity, Volume One* (New York, NY: Harper and Row, 1975), p. 45.

27 Probe Ministries. "Answering the Big Questions of Life." Date of Access: May 6, 2012 (http://www.probe.org/site/c. fdKEIMNsEoG/b.4223635/k.5E6A/Answering_the_ Big_Questions_of_Life.htm).

28 CBN. "What Makes the Christian Message Unique?" Date of Access: April 4, 2012 (http://www.cbn.com/spiritual-life/ChurchAndMinistry/Evangelism/What_Makes_the_ Christian_Message_Unique.aspx).

29 John Eldredge. Epic (Nashville, TN: Thomas Nelson, 2004), p. 15.

30 Francis A. Schaeffer. *Escape from Reason* (Downers Grove, IL: Intervarsity Press, 1968), p. 106.

31 H.J. Richards. *The Miracles of Jesus: What Really Happened?* (Mystic, CT: Twenty-Third Publishers, 1986), p. 101.

32 Ibid., p. 100.

33 The Universal Moral Code. "Universal Moral Code" Date of Access: June 6, 2012. (http://www.universalmoralcode.com).

34 Dictionary.com. "Conscience." Date of Access: December 24, 2012 (http://dictionary.reference.com/browse/Conscience?s=t)

www.ingramcontent.com/pod-product-compliance
Lightning Source LLC
Chambersburg PA
CBHW062101080426
42734CB00012B/2716